# The Balanced Life

The balanced life is a state of equally moderate-to-high levels of satisfaction in important and multiple life domains that contribute to overall life satisfaction. This book strives to improve the reader's understanding of what the balanced life is, and how it can be both achieved and maintained. Its primary goal is therefore to identify the major principles of life balance and to introduce a comprehensive construct of the balanced life reflective of these principles. It discusses how life balance substantially contributes to subjective wellbeing – defined as life satisfaction, a preponderance of positive over negative feelings, and absence of ill-being – and explores strategies to attain life balance. It argues that achieving life balance, through manipulating one's thoughts and taking concrete action, will lead to increased personal happiness. Aimed at professional, academic, and lay audiences, this book is grounded in scientific studies related to work-life balance and the balanced life.

M. JOSEPH SIRGY is a management psychologist. He has published extensively in the area of business administration, business ethics, and quality of life. He cofounded the International Society for Quality-of-Life Studies, the Macromarketing Society, and the Community Indicators Consortium. Over the years, he has received numerous awards for his research, teaching, and service to the management discipline.

# The Balanced Life

## Using Strategies from Behavioral Science to Enhance Wellbeing

M. JOSEPH SIRGY
*Virginia Polytechnic Institute and State University,*
*and North West University*

CAMBRIDGE
UNIVERSITY PRESS

# CAMBRIDGE
## UNIVERSITY PRESS

University Printing House, Cambridge CB2 8BS, United Kingdom

One Liberty Plaza, 20th Floor, New York, NY 10006, USA

477 Williamstown Road, Port Melbourne, VIC 3207, Australia

314–321, 3rd Floor, Plot 3, Splendor Forum, Jasola District Centre,
New Delhi – 110025, India

103 Penang Road, #05–06/07, Visioncrest Commercial, Singapore 238467

Cambridge University Press is part of the University of Cambridge.

It furthers the University's mission by disseminating knowledge in the pursuit of
education, learning, and research at the highest international levels of excellence.

www.cambridge.org
Information on this title: www.cambridge.org/9781009123242
DOI: 10.1017/9781009128544

First published 2022

*A catalogue record for this publication is available from the British Library.*

*Library of Congress Cataloging-in-Publication Data*
Names: Sirgy, M. Joseph, author.
Title: The balanced life : using strategies from behavioral science to enhance
wellbeing / M. Joseph Sirgy, Virginia Polytechnic Institute and State University.
Description: Cambridge, United Kingdom ; New York, NY : Cambridge
University Press, 2022. | Includes bibliographical references and index.
Identifiers: LCCN 2021059602 (print) | LCCN 2021059603 (ebook) |
ISBN 9781009123242 (hardback) | ISBN 9781009128544 (ebook)
Subjects: LCSH: Quality of life – Psychological aspects. | Work-life balance. |
Well-being. | BISAC: PSYCHOLOGY / Clinical Psychology
Classification: LCC HN25 .S529 2022 (print) |
LCC HN25 (ebook) | DDC 306.01/9–dc23/eng/20220210
LC record available at https://lccn.loc.gov/2021059602
LC ebook record available at https://lccn.loc.gov/2021059603

ISBN 978-1-009-12324-2 Hardback
ISBN 978-1-009-12454-6 Paperback

*This book is dedicated to my wife (Pamela), my four
children (Melissa, Danielle, Michelle, and Emmaline),
my five grandchildren (Isabella, Alexander, Scott, Jake,
and Luke), my two brothers (Abraham and Jimmy), and
my cousins and their families scattered in the United States,
Canada, Australia, France, Lebanon, and Egypt. The book
is also dedicated to all those wellbeing researchers who
have devoted much of their professional careers to the
promulgation of the science of wellbeing, happiness, and
quality of life – those who believe that there is more to life
than simply surviving or minimizing the stresses
and strains of daily life. Wellbeing, happiness, and
quality-of-life researchers shine a beacon of
light to the science that can elevate human
existence and make people flourish.*

# Contents

# Figures

# Tables

# Preface

Much research has documented concepts related to the balanced life in the literatures of organizational/industrial psychology and human resource management. These concepts include work-life balance, work–family conflict, work–family interference, and work–family interface (see literature reviews of various concepts related to work-life balance by Allen et al. [2000], Bulger and Fisher [2012], Byron [2005], Casper et al. [2007], Danna and Griffin [1999], Eby et al. [2005, 2010], Greenhaus and Allen [2011], Kalliath and Brough [2008], Kossek and Ozeki [1998], Lee and Sirgy [2017], McNall et al. [2010], Sirgy and Lee [2016, 2018], Sirgy et al. [2008], and Yasbek [2004]). In the literature on subjective wellbeing and quality of life, only a few studies were found that specifically addressed the concept of life balance. For example, Diener et al. (2008) reported a study involving a representative sample from around the world to assess people's affect balance (positive versus negative affect) on the previous day and the various activities they had engaged in. The study found that the most popular activity that most people engaged in was socializing with family and friends. In this context, the study also found a *decreasing marginal utility* of this type of activity. That is, to ensure an optimal level of life satisfaction, people attempted to engage in a variety of activities because satisfaction from one type of activity diminishes of time. Sheldon and Niemiec (2006) demonstrated that life balance is achieved not only by the fulfillment of psychological needs (needs for autonomy, competence, and relatedness) but also by a *balanced effect among the satisfaction of these needs*. Matuska (2012) conceptualized life balance as congruence between both desired and actual time spent in activities and equivalence in the degree of discrepancy between desired and actual time spent across *activities that satisfy basic and growth needs* (needs related to health, relationship, challenge/interest, and identity). The author was able to demonstrate a strong association between life balance and personal wellbeing. A similar conceptualization was introduced by Sheldon et al. (2010). They defined life balance as perceived low discrepancy between actual and ideal time-use profiles. The authors developed a life-balance measure on the basis of this conceptualization and were able to demonstrate that life balance is positively related to subjective wellbeing mediated by psychological need satisfaction.

I very briefly addressed the concept of the balanced life in my book *Psychology of Quality of Life* (Sirgy, 2002). In Chapter 14 of the book, titled "Balance," I proposed that people make attempts to create balance in their lives to *optimize* life satisfaction (i.e., achieve and maintain an acceptable level of life satisfaction). A distinction between two balance concepts was made: within-domain balance and between-domain balance. *Balance within a life domain* is achieved by striving to experience both positive and negative affects. Positive affect reflects a reward function, namely goals are attained and resources are acquired. In contrast, negative affect serves a motivational function. That is, negative affect helps an individual recognize problems and opportunities for future achievement and growth (cf. Kitayama & Markus, 2000). *Balance between life domains* can be achieved through compensation (i.e., increasing the salience of positive life domains compensates for negative life domains, and conversely, decreasing the salience of negative life domains helps reduce the influence of negative affect from these domains on overall life satisfaction) (see also Sirgy, 2012). I, with a doctoral student (Jiyun Wu), published an article titled "The Pleasant Life, the Engaged Life, and the Meaningful Life: What about the Balanced Life?" in the *Journal of Happiness Studies* (Sirgy & Wu, 2009). In this article, we positioned the concept of the balanced life vis-à-vis other popular concepts of subjective wellbeing, namely, "the pleasant life," "the engaged life," and "the meaningful life" (as proposed by Martin Seligman in his 2002 book *Authentic Happiness*). Seligman has argued that life satisfaction stems from three major sets of experiences in life, namely experiencing pleasantness regularly (the pleasant life), experiencing a high level of engagement in satisfying activities (the engaged life), and experiencing a sense of connectedness to a greater whole (the meaningful life). In response, we (Sirgy and Wu) countered by suggesting that having a balanced life is equally important to life satisfaction. The balanced life is experienced when people are highly engaged in social roles in multiple domains. We explained the effect of balance on life satisfaction using two concepts, namely *satisfaction limits* (i.e., people can derive only a limited amount of satisfaction from a single life domain; hence, engagement in multiple domains is necessary to optimize life satisfaction) and *satisfaction of the full spectrum of human developmental needs* (i.e., people have to be involved in multiple domains to satisfy both basic and growth needs; both sets of needs have to be met to induce a high level of subjective wellbeing). This article won the Best Paper award in the journal and was reprinted in *Explorations of Happiness* (edited by Delle Fave, 2013).

The goal of this book is to identify the major principles of life balance, and as such, I introduce to the reader a comprehensive construct of the balanced life reflective of these principles. To begin with, I describe how life balance contributes to subjective wellbeing (life satisfaction or perceived quality of life).

The balanced life is a state of equally moderate-to-high levels of satisfaction in important life domains contributing to overall life satisfaction. The balanced life can be achieved through a set of interdomain strategies. Two sets of interdomain strategies are identified, namely, strategies to prompt greater participation of satisfied domains to contribute to life satisfaction and strategies to increase domain satisfaction and decrease dissatisfaction.

Interdomain strategies designed to prompt greater participation of satisfied life domains to contribute to life satisfaction include: (1) engagement in social roles in multiple life domains (explained by the principle of satisfaction limits); (2) engagement in roles in health, safety, economic, social, work, leisure, and cultural domains (explained by the principle of satisfaction of the full spectrum of human development needs); and (3) engagement in new social roles (explained by the principle of diminishing satisfaction).

Interdomain strategies designed to increase domain satisfaction and decrease domain dissatisfaction include: (1) integrating domains with high satisfaction (explained by the principle of positive spillover), (2) compartmentalizing domains with low satisfaction (explained by the segmentation principle), (3) optimizing domain satisfaction by reallocating resources across domains (explained by the compensation principle), (4) stress management (explained by the principle of role conflict reduction), and (5) using skills, experiences, and resources in one role for other roles (explained by the principle of role enrichment).

I hope that by the time you have finished reading this book, you will walk away with a better understanding of what causes people to experience imbalance in their lives and conversely how to achieve or restore balance in your own life and the lives of others. Doing so should enhance your own quality of life and that of those people around you.

# Acknowledgments

My gratitude extends to David Repetto, Executive Publisher at Cambridge University Press, and his team: Santhamurthy Ramamoorthy, Natasha Whelan, Rowan Groat, Harry James Morris, and Emily Watton for an excellent job related to acquisition, review, copyediting, production, and marketing of the book. I am most grateful to Emmaline Smith, who critiqued and copy-edited the entire book. Her input was most valuable in revising and rerevising the book manuscript to meet the publisher's guidelines. I am equally grateful to all my colleagues and friends who interacted with me discussing this important topic. Among them are professors Dong-Jin Lee, Jiyun Wu, Mohsen Joshanloo, Grace B. Yu, Michael Bosnjak, Don Rahtz, Minyoung Kim, Ahmet Ekici, Anusorn Singhapakdi, and Eda Gurel-Atay.

I am additionally grateful to my family for moral support and love – my wife, Pamela Jackson, and my four daughters Melissa Racklin (her husband Anton Racklin and her four beautiful children, Isabella, Alec, Jake, and Luke), Danielle Barrick (her husband John and her son Scott), Michelle Sirgy, and Emmaline Smith. My many thanks are also extended to my two brothers, Abraham and Jimmy, and their families, as well as his many cousins and their families scattered in many places around the world.

# About the Author

M. *Joseph Sirgy* is a management psychologist (PhD, University of Massachusetts, 1979), the Virginia Tech Real Estate Professor Emeritus of Marketing at Virginia Polytechnic Institute and State University (USA), and Extraordinary Professor at North-West University, Potchefstroom Campus (South Africa). He has published extensively in the area of marketing, business ethics, and quality of life. He cofounded the International Society for Quality-of-Life Studies (ISQOLS) in 1995, served as its Executive Director/Treasurer from 1995 to 2011, and as Development Codirector (2011–present). In 1998, he received the Distinguished Fellow Award from ISQOLS. In 2003, ISQOLS honored him as the Distinguished Quality-of-Life Researcher for research excellence and a record of lifetime achievement in quality-of-life research. He also served as a president of the Academy of Marketing Science (2002–2004) from which he received the Distinguished Fellow Award in the early 1990s and the Harold Berkman Service Award in 2007 (lifetime achievement award for serving the marketing professoriate). In the early 2000s, he helped cofound the Macromarketing Society and the Community Indicators Consortium and has served as a board member of these two professional associations. He cofounded the journal *Applied Research in Quality of Life*, the official journal of the International Society for Quality-of-Life Studies, in 2005, and he has served as the cofounding editor (1995–present). He also served as the editor of the quality-of-life section in the *Journal of Macromarketing* (1995–2016). He received the Virginia Tech's Pamplin Teaching Excellence Award/Holtzman Outstanding Educator Award and University Certificate of Teaching Excellence in 2008. In 2010, ISQOLS honored him for excellence and lifetime service to society. In 2010, he won the Best Paper Award in the *Journal of Happiness Studies* for his theory of the balanced life; in 2011, he won the Best Paper Award in the *Journal of Travel Research* for his goal theory of leisure travel satisfaction. In 2012, he was awarded the EuroMed Management

Research Award for outstanding achievements and groundbreaking contributions to wellbeing and quality-of-life research. In 2019, the Macromarketing Society honored him with the Robert W. Nason Award for extraordinary and sustained contributions to the field of macromarketing. He is currently serving as Editor-in-Chief of the *Journal of Macromarketing* (2020–present). He also was the editor of ISQOLS/Springer book series on *International Handbooks in QOL* (2008–2015), *Community QOL Indicators: Best Cases* (2004–2015), and *Applied Research in QOL: Best Practices* (2008–2012). He is currently the coeditor of Springer's book series titled *Human Well-Being and Policy Making* (2015–present).

His recent books include:

- Sirgy, M. Joseph (2021). *The Psychology of Quality of Life: Wellbeing and Positive Mental Health*. 3rd ed. Dordrecht: Springer Publishing.
- Sirgy, M. Joseph (2020). *Positive Balance: A Theory of Well-Being and Positive Mental Health*. Dordrecht: Springer Publishing.
- Sirgy, M. Joseph, Richard J. Estes, El-Sayed El-Aswad, and Don R. Rahtz (2019). *Combatting Jihadist Terrorism through Nation Building: A Quality-of-Life Perspective*. Dordrecht: Springer Publishing.
- Estes, Richard J. and M. Joseph Sirgy (2018). *Advances in Well-Being: Toward a Better World*. London: Rowman & Littlefield.
- Uysal, Muzaffer, Stefan Kruger, and M. Joseph Sirgy (Eds.) (2018). *Managing Quality of Life in Tourism and Hospitality: Best Practices*. Oxfordshire: CABI Publishers.
- Estes, Richard J. and M. Joseph Sirgy (Eds.) (2017). *The Pursuit of Well-Being: The Untold Global History*. Dordrecht: Springer Publishing.
- Sirgy, M. Joseph, Rhonda Phillips, and Don Rahtz (Eds.) (2013). *Community Quality-of-Life Indicators: Best Cases VI*. Dordrecht: Springer Publishing.
- Sirgy, M. Joseph (2012). *The Psychology of Quality of Life: Hedonic Well-Being, Life Satisfaction, and Eudaimonia*. 2nd edition. Dordrecht: Springer Publishing.
- Reilly, Nora P., M. Joseph Sirgy, and C. Allen Gorman (Eds.) (2012). *Work and Quality of Life: Ethical Practices in Organizations*. Dordrecht: Springer Publishing.

- Uysal, Muzaffer, Richard Perdue, and M. Joseph Sirgy (Eds.) (2012). *Handbook of Tourism and Quality-of-Life Research: Enhancing the Lives of Tourists and Residents.* Dordrecht: Springer Publishing.
- Land, Kenneth C., Alex C. Michalos, and M. Joseph Sirgy (Eds.) (2012). *Handbook of Social Indicators and Quality-of-Life Research.* Dordrecht: Springer Publishing.

# PART I

# Introduction

An important aspect of the balanced life is balance between work life and nonwork life. We have seen a dramatic increase in the number of working women in the labor force (e.g., Percheski, 2008). This increase has resulted in a fundamental shift in family structure – away from a structure characterized by the husband being the breadwinner and the wife being the homemaker and toward a structure reflective of a dual-career couple (e.g., Sayer, 2005). While modern couples are more likely to have both parties in the workforce, it is equally true that unmarried women are also in the workforce in large numbers, and more men are staying home as caregivers than in recent history. As a result, working men and women have increasingly faced significant demands at work and at home, causing imbalance and conflict between work and nonwork domains, which in turn plays an important role in the quality of life (e.g., Eby et al., 2005; Williams, Berdahl, & Vandello, 2016).

This book explores the concept of life balance, a concept at the heart of the science wellbeing, its essential condition, and its *sine qua non*. Let us first define the concept of balance. The etymology of "balance" derives from the Latin *bilanx*, which denotes two (*bi*) scale pans (*lanx*). The word involves a dialectical relationship that could be spectral (between poles of a spectrum, such as hot versus cold) or categorical (between dichotomous categories that are often associated with each other, such as work and life). Balance could also be synchronic – balance involving a variable in each situation at a given moment, such as homeostatic equilibrium regarding temperature (balance between cold and hot in each situation at a given moment). In contrast, balance could involve a long-term situation over time, such as a work-life balance (Pollock et al., 2000). However, in many instances, the word "balance" is usually qualified by the use of "optimal balance." For example, the ancient Greek philosopher, Aristotle, views optimal balance as an ideal point, which in some circumstances may be toward one of the two poles – it is the "golden mean" (Telfer, 1989). It should be noted that optimal balance does not involve some calculation of the midpoint on a spectrum. To better understand optimal balance, let us consider a related concept, namely the Swedish notion of *lagom* – a state involving just the *right amount* (Dunne, 2017). As such, much of this book addresses the concept of balanced life from the vantage point of optimal balance, an ideal point, or the right amount of balance – the degree of balance most likely to secure an optimal level of wellbeing.

This book is divided into three major parts. Part I introduces the reader to basic concepts of life balance and imbalance. Specifically, I provide the reader with a little history of the concept of work-life balance and make the case of why this concept is very important in contemporary society. I also discuss the imbalanced life and those factors that lead to imbalance – situational, personal, organizational, and societal factors. Parts II and III expose the reader to specific concepts of life balance, concepts related to how people using their own thoughts and action manage to create balance in their lives. Hence, the focus of this book is how to create life balance by manipulating one's own thoughts and actions, which is different from institutional policies and programs designed to create balance. That is, much has been written about policies designed to increase work-life balance. Examples include the right to maternity leave, paternity leave, sick leave, minimum wage, healthcare, and so on. These are government policies designed to enhance life balance. The same thing can be said about institutional programs. Many organizations have designed and implemented work-life balance programs in the context of their own organizations and communities. Examples include fitness programs, childcare programs, elderly care programs, and health-related educational programs, among many others. This book is not about institutional policies and programs related to work-life balance. This book focuses on what people do (and can do) to increase the likelihood of creating balance in their lives using their own thoughts and actions, not relying on institutional policies and programs.

What do I mean by "creating life balance using one's own thoughts and actions"? Much of this book addresses the psychology related to how people segment their emotional experiences in life domains. People's feelings are segmented in life spheres such as work life, family life, spiritual life, financial life, love life, leisure life, intellectual life, and so on. For example, most people can easily respond to survey questions concerning how satisfied they are about their "love life," "family life," "social life," etc. This is indicative of the fact that people indeed organize their emotional experiences in "life domains" and can articulate how they feel overall about many domains. The idea of life balance through thoughts and actions reflects how people do things (mentally and physically) to manipulate their emotional experiences in life domains for the purpose of maintaining an acceptable level of life satisfaction. This manipulation involves the interplay between and among the life domains. This is what I am calling "interdomain strategies." Part II of this book exposes the reader to interdomain strategies designed to prompt greater participation of life domains vested with a preponderance of positive feelings that contribute to overall life satisfaction. Examples of these interdomain strategies include engagement in social roles across multiple domains. This means getting more involved in a variety of domains that can increase your overall happiness in life. Take for example persons who spend most of their days and possibly nights working on professional projects, they find fulfilling. This is not necessarily a good thing for their overall happiness in life. To increase their happiness, they should "have a life." That is, they should be involved not only in their work life, but they also need a social life, a family life, a spiritual life, etc. "Putting all their eggs in one basket" doesn't help increase their overall personal happiness. As such, Part II of this book discusses how people who are happier in life tend to be involved in multiple domains and experience positive emotions by satisfying the full spectrum of human development needs – basic needs such as health and safety and growth needs such as relatedness to others, competence, and autonomy.

In contrast, Part III discusses interdomain strategies people use to increase satisfaction and decrease dissatisfaction in specific life domains. For example, people create balance in their lives by integrating their work and family domains when they have positive feelings in both their work life and family life. Integrating work and family domains serve to amplify their positive feelings in both domains, which in turn contribute more significantly to their overall happiness. A married team managing their own business through their home is perhaps the ultimate form of domain integration. On the other hand, many people choose to segment their life domains. That is, they create impermeable boundaries between their work life and family life. They do so when they experience immense negativity at work, and they don't want that negativity to spill over to the family life. Therefore, they compartmentalize their work life and insulate it to protect their family life from getting "infected" by the toxicity they experience in their work life. This is another interdomain strategy. Again, the goal of these types of strategies is to help increase satisfaction in a domain, protect a domain from diminishing satisfaction, or prevent a domain from increasing dissatisfaction.

# 1 | *Life Balance*
*Setting the Stage and*
*Understanding the Language*

## A Little History

Issues of work-life balance have gained prominence over the last several decades. This may be due to the changing aspects of work and non-work life (Lockwood, 2003; Naithani, 2010; Voydanoff, 2006). We can trace the changing aspects of work and nonwork life to communal living in the preindustrial period (see Table 1.1). Preindustrial societies, referred to as communal living, often involved the entire family working for subsistence at home or near home (frequently via subsistence farming) and where the home was the center of production.

By the mid-eighteenth century, increasing population demands coupled with the rise of new technology ushered in the Industrial Revolution across Europe and replaced largely rural, agrarian communities with growing urban centers. Masses of workers migrated to factories for jobs in the cities, which meant that work moved from outside of the home sphere for the first time for many. This manufacturing trend, also known as the factory system, produced a situation in which men dominated the workforce in factories, whereas women dominated the household. As such, the division of labor based on gender significantly increased during the late eighteenth and early nineteenth centuries. Men had an advantage over women in operating heavy equipment in manufacturing plants, exacerbating the division of labor based on gender. This meant that, in urban centers, it was common for men to work in manufacturing plants, whereas women more frequently concentrated on housework and raising families.

However, technology introduced in the 1950s played an important role in the division of labor based on gender roles. Physical strength, typically men's forte, was replaced by technology, allowing women to participate in the workplace at an accelerated rate. This trend set the stage for the introduction of work-life balance programs and policies in many firms. The 1980s and 1990s witnessed

Table 1.1 *Changing aspects of work and nonwork life*

| Time period | Changes in aspects of work and nonwork life |
|---|---|
| Preindustrial period or communal living (decades directly preceding the Industrial Revolution) | The whole family is engaged in work for subsistence at home or near home, largely agrarian |
| Industrial Revolution (c. 1760s–1840s) | Work life is segmented from nonwork life; men dominated the workplace, making work life highly salient for men; and conversely, family life is highly salient for women |
| Late 1700s–early 1800s | Further segregation between work and family life due to the division of labor based on gender roles |
| Early 1800s–1950 | Technology abetted male dominance in the workplace |
| 1950s–early 1980s | Technology helped reverse gender division reversed; introduction of work-life balance policies and programs |
| 1980s–2008 | Increased labor participation by women and mothers; significant growth of policies and programs of work-life balance |
| 2008 onward | Increased challenges related to work-life balance due to working long hours, the rise of the service sector, the use of technology in the workplace, a growing aging population, the loss of social support networks, greater use of mobile technology, greater financial pressure, and increased pandemics |

*Source:* Adapted from research by Naithani (2010) and Voydanoff (2006).

an increasing number of organizations developing work-life balance policies and offering programs primarily aimed toward supporting working mothers. By the early part of the twenty-first century, such programs evolved into less gender-specific programs to address areas of life other than family life (i.e., social life, leisure life, financial life, and health and fitness). Beginning in the 1950s up to the early part of the twenty-first century, a wide array of factors influenced work and nonwork life (Naithani & Jha, 2009). Factors related to family and personal life included:

- increased participation of women in the labor market,
- increased participation of mothers in the labor market,
- increased participation of dual-career couples in the labor market,
- increased participation of single parents in the labor market,
- increased financial burden of childcare and eldercare, and
- increased awareness and importance of issues related to health and wellbeing.

Work-related factors included:

- increased work demand and resulting work–family conflict and stress,
- a culture demanding long hours at work and time squeeze – or decreased discretionary time,
- a trend toward seeking and accepting part-time employment as a means to cope with work-life imbalance, and
- a trend toward flexible scheduling.

Accompanying the increased participation of women in the labor market, dual-earner couples and single-parent households also increased their participation in the workforce. This trend resulted in greater demand for childcare and elderly care centers. However, the cost associated with these facilities was high, posing a significant financial burden on workers. More pressure was placed on management in organizations to develop work-life balance programs to help alleviate the financial burden. Beginning from the 1950s, workers began to be expected to work for more hours to meet increased work demand. This increased work demand resulted in greater work–family conflict and stress, which in turn placed more pressure on organizations to help deal with issues of work-life imbalance. Conflict between work and personal life was further exacerbated by the trend of working long hours, the rise of the service sector, the use of technology in the workplace, a growing aging population, the loss of social support networks, the use of mobile technology blurring the line between home and work life, greater financial pressure in raising a family, and increased public health crises.

Consider how the work-life balance has changed in the era of the COVID-19 pandemic (Daley, 2021). A recent survey conducted in the United Kingdom indicates that many feel fortunate to still have jobs, work-life boundaries have collapsed, and there is an increased fear of management employing remote surveillance of employees. This fear seems to have led to people working harder and longer hours. Employees who juggle work and home responsibilities seem to be struggling the most. Those who are taking care of their aging parents, the "sandwich generation," are also struggling.

## Why Is Work-Life Balance Important?

The research literature on work-life balance is very rich. Since the 1950s, work-life balance researchers have published a phenomenal number of studies that have clearly demonstrated the detrimental effects of work–family conflict on job and life satisfaction (e.g., Kossek & Ozeki, 1998) and the benefits of work-life programs for both employers and employees (e.g., Byrne, 2005; Hewlett et al., 2005; Hudson, 2005, 2006; McDonald & Bradley, 2005). Though work-life balance programs are often company specific, a few common examples of such programs are flextime, vouchers for fitness centers, vouchers for childcare, and vouchers for elderly care. The benefits of work-life balance programs are wide ranging to include social and psychological as well as economic benefits (see Table 1.2). Thus, the management of large and small organizations has jumped on the bandwagon to establish its own work-life programs to enhance employee productivity and organizational profitability.

Consider the following case study. Yeandle et al. (2006) analyzed the effects of instituting a work-life balance program at British Telecom. The work-life balance researchers noted that, in 2006, British Telecom employed 102,000 workers. The firm established a work-life balance program involving work flexibility; specifically, 75,000 workers were given flexible work hours. The benefits of this work-life balance program were demonstrably positive. Specifically, the productivity yield from this program was estimated at approximately 21 percent, which translated into £6 million. The annual staff turnover was reduced to below 4 percent compared with 17 percent of the sector at large. Absenteeism was reduced to less than three days per person per annum. Customer satisfaction also increased: 20 million customers rated quality of service at 5 percent higher (and satisfaction at 7 percent higher) than that before the implementation of the work flexibility program.

Table 1.2 *Benefits of work-life balance programs for employers and employees*

| Benefits for employers | Benefits for employees |
| --- | --- |
| Work-life balance programs help employers by:<br>• Retaining valued employees<br>• Motivating employees to excel in job performance<br>• Attracting more and better job candidates<br>• Enhancing the overall reputation of the organization<br>• Reducing the costs of employee recruitment<br>• Reducing the costs of employee absenteeism and presenteeism<br>• Reducing the costs of diminished productivity<br>• Reducing the costs of employee turnover<br>• Reducing the costs of health insurance premiums<br>• Reducing the costs of employee medical claims<br>• Reducing the costs associated with customer dissatisfaction | Work-life balance programs help employees by:<br>• Increasing satisfaction in work and nonwork life<br>• Enhancing interpersonal relationships in the workplace<br>• Enhancing self-esteem<br>• Allowing more time to meet demand in family life<br>• Enhancing work-related self-efficacy<br>• Improving management of work and family life<br>• Providing support to manage problems at work and home |

Researchers were also able to demonstrate positive financial returns to companies with work-life balance programs. Watson (2002) presented evidence, suggesting a relationship between work-life balance programs and organizational financial performance. Specifically, companies with work-life balance programs were reported to have a higher market value than those with no work-life balance programs. Evidence also suggests that organizations with work-life balance programs tend to experience greater growth in their market value than those with no such programs.

The most obvious organizational benefits include increased job performance, employee productivity, job satisfaction, employee morale,

and organizational loyalty and commitment. Besides these, other organizational benefits are related to reductions in organizational costs.
Organizational costs, such as health-related costs,[1] can be reduced
through work-life balance initiatives. Now, consider the following study
findings. It is estimated that employers in the United States have lost
$150 billion per year in employees' direct and indirect health-related
costs (Golden & Jorgensen, 2002). Additionally, the costs of employee
absenteeism in Canada have been estimated to be up to $10 billion a year
(Duxbury & Higgins, 2003).

## Theoretical Notions

To follow the subsequent discussion, the reader needs to become
familiar with some basic concepts of subjective wellbeing, namely life
domain, domain satisfaction, the bottom-up spillover process of life
satisfaction, and role theory. To understand the psychology related
to the bottom-up spillover process of life satisfaction and role theory,
the reader can benefit from a discussion related to "life domain" and
"domain satisfaction." Then, we will tackle the concept of "balance."

Andrews and Withey (1976) were the earliest proponents of the
life-domain approach to the study of quality of life and subjective
wellbeing. These researchers used statistical techniques, such as multiple regression, to predict survey respondents' life satisfaction scores
("How do you feel about life as a whole?" with responses captured on
a 7-point delighted–terrible scale). They found that satisfaction with
various life domains explained much of the variation in life satisfaction scores. These domains were interpersonal relations, self, family,
leisure/leisure-time activities, home, friends and associates, neighborhood, job, education, services/facilities, community, economic
situation, local government, national government, and contemporary life in the United States. Around the same time in 1976, another
team of researchers (Campbell et al., 1976) used a similar set of life
domains, namely leisure/nonworking activities, family, standard of
living, work, marriage, savings/investments, friendships, city/county,

---

[1] Healthcare costs are reduced when the insurance company observes decreased
healthcare expenditure on employees' healthcare (as paid by the insurance company). Reduction in healthcare expenditure prompts a decrease in the premium
that the organization pays to the insurance company.

housing, education, neighborhood, life in the United States, health, religion, national government, and organizations. Many other quality-of-life/wellbeing researchers have uncovered other variations of life domains (see literature reviews by Diener [1984], Diener et al. [1999], and Sirgy [2012]), and the notion of satisfaction in life domains contributing to a life satisfaction judgment has come to be known as the *bottom-up spillover theory of life satisfaction.*

In the second part of the book, specifically in Chapters 4 and 5, I will be zeroing in on a set of life domains I believe are most pertinent to the question of the balanced life. These seven life domains are love life, family life, material life, social life, work life, leisure life, and cultural life. Affective experiences are stored in memory in life spheres, and these spheres are organized in a hierarchy of satisfaction. At the top of the satisfaction hierarchy is life satisfaction – a hot cognition (a belief associated with strong feelings), reflecting how the individual feels about his/her life overall. Second in line in the satisfaction hierarchy is domain satisfaction. That is, people make judgments about how they feel in certain life domains, such as family life, social life, work life, material life, and community life. Satisfaction in these life domains influences the life satisfaction judgment, which is at the top of the satisfaction hierarchy – the most abstract hot cognition. At the bottom of the satisfaction hierarchy are concrete hot cognitions related to satisfaction with specific life events (i.e., concrete and salient events that have occurred and are associated with positive or negative affect). As such, satisfaction judgments related to life events (most concrete hot cognitions) influence satisfaction judgments of life domains, which in turn influence satisfaction with life overall (most abstract hot cognition). The reader should then note that the central tenet of bottom-up spillover theory of life satisfaction is the carryover of affect from subordinate life domains to superordinate ones, specifically from life domains, such as leisure, family, job, and health, to overall life satisfaction. Thus, bottom-up spillover implies that subjective wellbeing (or life satisfaction) can be increased by allowing life domains to carry positive feelings or satisfaction to spill over into the most superordinate domain (overall life). The positive affect accumulates in life domains as a direct function of satisfaction of human development needs – physiological needs, safety needs, social needs, esteem needs, self-actualization needs, knowledge needs, and aesthetic needs (Maslow, 1970).

Another theory that may help the reader better understand how people use their own thoughts and actions to create a balanced life is role theory (Kahn et al., 1964; Katz & Kahn, 1978). Role theory posits that work and nonwork roles (e.g., family roles) are associated with role expectations – the expectations of others or what is believed to be appropriate behavior for a particular role (e.g., coworker, spouse, and father). Both work and nonwork domains entail multiple roles in which the individual experiences role demands, ultimately resulting in role conflict. Work and nonwork domains can be incompatible because we have limited resources (time, energy, money, etc.), and we expend those resources trying to meet role demand to ensure optimal role performance.[2] Increased role performance in one domain (such as work) may result in decreased role performance in another domain (such as family). Consequently, role conflict reflects role demand from the work and nonwork domains that may be mutually incompatible because of resource limitations. Numerous research has used role theory to conceptualize and test models of work–family conflict[3] – models involving antecedents, consequences, mediators, and moderators involving the construct of work–family conflict. For an enlightening discussion of work–family conflict, see Michel et al. (2009, 2011), Fiksenbaum (2014), and Liao et al. (2019).

Having explained the concepts of life domains, domain satisfaction, and role conflict, the reader is now ready to appreciate the discussion concerning how people manipulate the interplay between

---

[2] There is another theory in the work-life balance literature called *conservation of resources* (Grandey & Cropanzano, 1999; Hobfoll, 1989, 2001; Hobfoll & Freedy, 1993). The theory posits that people strive to obtain, retain, protect, and foster resources they value. When they are forced to use all their resources on work matters, they end up with less resources on nonwork concerns, such as family matters. As such, they may experience emotional exhaustion, depression, and burnout, trying to juggle both work and nonwork roles. The more conflict is experienced in one domain, the less resources are available to meet role demands in another domain (Jensen, 2016).

[3] The reader can better appreciate the concept of work–family conflict by knowing how industrial/organizational psychologists measure family-to-work interference (FWI) and work-to-family interference (WFI). Here is an example of FWI: "My family life kept me from spending the amount of time I would like to spend on my job or career-related activities." An example of WFI is: "My job kept me from spending the amount of time that I would like to spend with my family" (Carlson & Frone, 2003).

life domains (and roles within life domains) and domain satisfaction to increase life balance, which in turn contributes to life satisfaction. That is, to achieve life balance, people engage in behavioral strategies to increase life satisfaction by manipulating the interplay among domain satisfaction to prompt greater participation of satisfied life domains to contribute to life satisfaction and increase domain satisfaction and decrease domain dissatisfaction. That is, life balance can be achieved by allowing those life domains containing a great deal of positive feelings (i.e., high levels of domain satisfaction) to influence how one feels about life at large (i.e., high levels of life satisfaction). More specifically, interdomain strategies designed to amplify the impact of satisfied life domains on overall life satisfaction and achieve balance include: (1) engagement in social roles in multiple life domains (explained by the principle of satisfaction limits); (2) engagement in roles in health, safety, economic, social, work, leisure, and cultural domains (explained by the principle of satisfaction of the full spectrum of human development needs); and (3) engagement in new social roles (explained by the principle of diminishing satisfaction). The other set of behavioral strategies to achieve life balance involves what a person does in the context of specific life domains to increase satisfaction (and decrease dissatisfaction) in those domains. As such, interdomain strategies designed to increase domain satisfaction and decrease domain dissatisfaction include: (1) integrating domains with high satisfaction (explained by the principle of positive spillover); (2) compartmentalizing domains with low satisfaction (explained by the segmentation principle); (3) reallocating resources life domains (explained by the compensation principle); (4) minimizing role conflict (explained by the principle of role strain and stress); and (5) using skills, experiences, and resources in one role for other roles (explained by the principle of role enrichment).

I will begin by discussing those principles related to prompting greater participation of satisfied life domains to contribute to life satisfaction (see Figure 1.1). However, before jumping right into those psychological strategies people use to achieve life balance, let's first address the concept of life imbalance and the common factors causing imbalance, after which we'll focus on strategies people use to achieve balance.

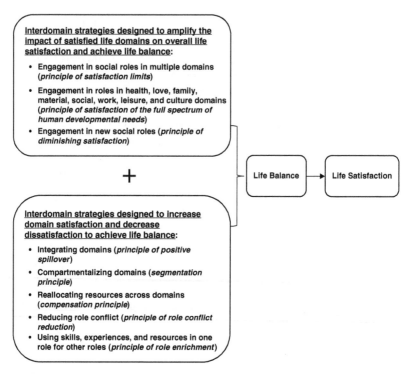

**Figure 1.1** Behavioral strategies of life balance

## Summary and Conclusion

I started the chapter by providing the reader with a little history of the work-life balance movement, focusing mostly on the last two centuries – tracing the changing aspects of work and nonwork life from communal living in the preindustrial period to 2008 onward. Communal living, or preindustrial society, reflected the common situation in which the whole family is engaged in work for subsistence at or near the home. Typically, families were engaged in agrarian work where the home was the center of production. However, during the Industrial Revolution of the mid-eighteenth to mid-nineteenth centuries, work life became segmented from nonwork life with the rise of the factory system. Division of labor along gender lines further reinforced segregation between work and family life during this period. As such, men dominated the workplace, making work life highly salient for men and, conversely, family life in the home sphere highly salient for women. Between 1950 and the early

1980s, we witnessed an increased adoption of technology in the workplace that helped reverse gender division. Work-life balance programs and policies were first introduced during this period. Then, we witnessed increased labor participation by women and mothers between 1980 and 2008. Work-life balance programs and policies picked up momentum and became increasingly popular. However, more recently, we have been witnessing increased challenges related to work-life balance, especially during public health crises such as the COVID-19 pandemic.

I spoke of the importance of the concept of work-life balance. The benefits of work-life balance programs are wide ranging to include social and psychological as well as economic benefits. Researchers were also able to demonstrate positive financial returns to companies with work-life balance programs. Evidence also suggests that organizations with work-life balance programs tend to experience greater growth in their market value than firms with no programs. Other benefits include increased job performance, employee productivity, job satisfaction, employee morale, and organizational loyalty and commitment. Work-life balance programs also serve to reduce organizational costs such as health-related costs.

To help the reader better understand the language involving the psychology of the balanced life, I introduced the reader to basic concepts of subjective wellbeing, life domains, domain satisfaction, the bottom-up spillover process of life satisfaction, and role theory. Domain satisfaction is a core concept in the psychology of the balanced life. Much research has shown that satisfaction in salient life domains (satisfaction with social life, work life, financial life, family life, love life, etc.) plays a very important role in determining life satisfaction overall. Satisfaction with specific life events contributes to domain satisfaction. The notion of satisfaction in life domains (i.e., domain satisfaction) influencing how people evaluate their life overall (i.e., life satisfaction) has come to be known as the *bottom-up spillover theory of life satisfaction*. That is, affective experiences (i.e., positive and negative feelings) are stored in memory in life domains, and these domains become organized hierarchically (i.e., satisfaction hierarchy). At the top of the satisfaction hierarchy is life satisfaction – a hot cognition reflecting how the individual feels about his/her life overall. Second in line in the satisfaction hierarchy is domain satisfaction. That is, people make judgments about how they feel in certain life domains, such as family life, social life, work life, material life, and community life. Satisfaction in these life domains influences how people evaluate their lives overall (i.e., life satisfaction), which is at the top of the satisfaction hierarchy – the most abstract hot cognition. At the bottom of the satisfaction hierarchy are concrete hot cognitions related to satisfaction with specific life events. These are concrete and salient events stored in memory and are associated with positive or negative feelings. As such, satisfaction judgments related to life events (most concrete hot cognitions at the bottom of the satisfaction hierarchy) influence satisfaction judgments of life domains (domain satisfaction), which in turn influence life satisfaction (most abstract hot cognition in the satisfaction hierarchy).

I also discussed role theory, given the fact that it plays an important role in the psychology of the balanced life. Role theory posits that work and nonwork roles (e.g., family roles) are associated with role expectations – the expectations of others or what is believed to be appropriate behavior for a particular role (e.g., coworker, spouse, and father). Both work and nonwork domains entail multiple roles in which the individual experiences role demands, ultimately resulting in role conflict. Work and nonwork domains can be incompatible because we have limited resources (time, energy, money, etc.), and we expend those resources trying to meet role demand to ensure optimal role performance. Increased role performance in one domain (such as work) may result in decreased role performance in another domain (such as family). Consequently, role conflict reflects role demand from the work and nonwork domains that may be mutually incompatible because of resource limitation.

# 2 | *The Imbalanced Life*

*Life balance* is a very important social issue. We know from research that life balance plays an important role in personal wellbeing (Sirgy & Wu, 2009); conversely, imbalance wreaks havoc on personal wellbeing. But what is worse about life imbalance is that it not only wreaks havoc on personal wellbeing but also the wellbeing of others, those with whom the individual regularly interacts. This "contagion" is referred to in the work-life balance literature as *crossover* (van Emmerik et al., 2015; Westman, Brough, & Kalliath, 2009).

Life imbalance is often caused by a host of different drivers and conditions. I have organized these drivers and conditions into four categories, which I will discuss in this chapter: (1) situational, (2) personal, (3) organizational, and (4) societal (see Table 2.1).

## Situational Factors

One possible contributing factor to life imbalance is *role overload*. When people experience role overload in one domain, they shift to another domain and use resources from that domain to deal with the role overload. For example, when an individual experiences work overload at work (i.e., too much work with hard deadlines), (s)he brings the work home and uses family time and other resources to get the job done (Goode, 1960). In the preceding example, when that individual works at home to get his/her job done (family-to-work transition), (s)he has taken time from the family domain. This interdomain transition is considered a coping mechanism that alleviates role overload; however, the same mechanism tends to increase work–family conflict (Matthews, Swody, & Barnes-Farrell, 2011; Matthews, Winkel, & Wayne, 2014). Trying to deal with role overload in one domain by using resources from another domain tends to create life imbalance because such behavior drains resources from other domains leading to emotional exhaustion (Wayne et al., 2017).

Table 2.1 *Example factors that may cause life imbalance*

| Factors that contribute to life imbalance | Examples |
| --- | --- |
| Situational factors | Life imbalance occurs when people use resources in one life domain at the expense of other domains. |
| Personal factors | Life imbalance occurs for individuals with priority ideology, strong role identity, and maladaptive perfectionism. |
| Organizational factors | Life imbalance occurs for individuals with managerial positions, those working in organizations that have workplace policies or norms that prompt boundary flexibility, and those with nonsupportive supervisors. |
| Societal factors | Life imbalance occurs in transitioning economies where work-to-family conflict is likely to be high, especially in countries with traditional gender roles, compared to the economically developed countries with more egalitarian gender roles. |

For example, Jane is working as an IT technician in a large corporation. The company is experiencing a cybersecurity breach. Her immediate supervisor is demanding that his staff work extra hours to deal with the security breach. Jane takes work home to meet work demands. She does this for several months. She not only gives up her family time but her social life suffers as well. She does not have time to engage in her usual leisure and recreation sports, such as going to the gym to do yoga. She used to take care of her daughter's every need – fix her breakfast, take her to school, get together with other parents at school to help out, fix dinner after school, and spend family time with her daughter helping with homework. Now, because of the increased work demand, her husband has reluctantly picked up the slack. He is now complaining that he is failing to meet the hard deadlines imposed on him by his boss. Jane is now emotionally exhausted. Her family life is unraveling. She is beginning to feel depressed. She began making professional mistakes, and her work is now faltering because she is exhausted. So, you see in Jane's situation, in the short term, she was able to use family resources to meet work demand, and in the short run, she was able to deliver what her boss expected. Of course, meeting work demand made her boss happy, which in turn made her feel happy at work, leading to increased job satisfaction. However, in the long term, meeting work demand by using resources from her family life took an emotional toll, which, in the final analysis, negatively impacted Jane's work. Making mistakes at work (decreased job performance) made her boss unhappy, which made her feel unhappy too (decreased job satisfaction).

There is a well-established theory in industrial/organizational psychology referred to as *boundary theory* (Ashforth, Kreiner, & Fugate, 2000). This theory maintains that individuals erect boundaries between life domains (e.g., boundary between work life and family life). Some people in some situations treat these boundaries "flexibly." That is, they establish and frequently use gateways to leave one domain (i.e., work) and enter another (i.e., family). These boundaries can be physical or mental or a combination of both. The goal is to meet role demand without experiencing role overload (Matthews & Barnes-Farrell, 2010; Matthews, Swody, & Barnes-Farrell, 2011). This is referred to in the literature as "the principle of boundary flexibility." For example, an individual must deliver a report to his/her supervisor by a certain deadline. (S)he realizes that (s)he cannot meet the deadline given the limited hours of the day at work. (S)he needs more time. (S)he crosses over to the family domain by bringing his/her work material into his/her home and spends much of his/her time and energy at home trying to complete the report by the set deadline. Being able to do so hinges on the extent to which the boundaries between work life and family life are flexible (i.e., can be modified).

Let's face it. We have a finite set of resources (time, energy, money, etc.). These resources are used to meet demand in various life domains. For example, one has only so much time in each day. Spending time with family must come at the expense of spending time at work, and vice versa. That is, investment of resources to meet work demand depletes resources available for other life domains (family, social, leisure, sports and recreation, financial, spiritual, life, etc.). Life imbalance occurs when people use resources in one life domain at the expense of other domains. Coping with role overload in one life domain (e.g., work demand) by crossing over to another life domain (e.g., family life) and attempting to meet that demand in the other domain helps solve the immediate problem. But doing so creates life imbalance in the long run – as this takes away needed resources from the other domain. However, the reader should note that I have an entire chapter (Chapter 6) dedicated to integration strategies (i.e., how people integrate life domains in ways to generate additional positive emotions). So please don't get the impression that flexible boundaries between life domains are "bad" in the sense that they may lead to life imbalance. Yes, boundary flexibility can cause life imbalance, but people can counter the life imbalance effects by using integration strategies, especially given certain conditions (situational, personal, and societal conditions). Stay tuned!

### Personal Factors

Leslie, King, and Clair (2019) proposed that individuals vary in their *priority ideology* – beliefs regarding the importance of different life domains. For example, at one extreme, individuals with a strong work priority ideology believe that their work is more important than their personal life. As such, work demands have precedence over personal life demands. At the other extreme, individuals with a strong personal life priority ideology believe that their personal life is more important than their work life. As such, personal life demands have precedence over work life demands. Individuals with extreme priority ideology are very likely to experience life imbalance much more compared to individuals with moderate priority ideology. As we will see later, life balance is achieved when people experience the full spectrum of human development needs – needs related to biological sustenance, shelter and security, social and affection, esteem and achievement, self-actualization, and knowledge and creativity. These needs are not likely to be satisfied when people become totally immersed in certain domains (e.g., work life, family life) while neglecting others. Meeting the full spectrum of human development needs requires engagement in multiple life domains with at least a minimal level of involvement in these domains. As such, people with extreme priority ideology are likely to invest the majority of their time and energy only in domains that reflect their priority ideology. For example, a person who has a "work" priority ideology is most likely to invest much of his/her time and energy in work life. Such a strategy is likely to generate satisfaction in their work life by meeting esteem and achievement-related needs (which in turn would serve to meet other economic needs related to biological sustenance and security); however, at the same time, the same strategy is likely to be a cause of frustration in meeting other needs related to family, sociability, love, affection, belonging, leisure, and culture, among others.

A similar line of reasoning applies to *role identity*. People identify themselves with certain roles. An individual who strongly identifies with the family role regards that role as more salient. In doing so, s(he) adopts rules that ensure the primacy of family aspects in making work–family decisions (Greenhaus & Powell, 2006). The same goes for an individual who identifies him/herself in terms of his/her work. That is, that person is likely to adopt rules to ensure the primacy of work aspects in making work–family decisions. As such, making decisions about allocating work–family resources may be influenced by role identity. In other words, a strong work role identity is likely to motivate the individual to cross the family boundary and allocate family resources to meet work demand. And conversely, a strong family role identity is likely to motivate the individual to cross the work boundary and allocate work resources to meet family demand (Furtado, Sobral, & Peci, 2016; Matthews, Swody, & Barnes-Farrell, 2011). Again, those with strong role identities are likely to experience life imbalance because they tend to allocate much more resources to those roles they strongly identify with at the expense of other roles.

The reader should note that life imbalance is not restricted to work life versus some other life domain, such as family life. It can occur in relation to any life domain in which role identity usurps time and energy at the expanse from other domains. Consider a person whose identity is linked to politics, and this is an important domain in this individual's life. In other words, (s)he is a political activist. (S)he thinks of himself/herself as a political activist (his/her actual self), (s)he has an ideal self of becoming more politically engaged (his/her ideal self), people around him/her perceive him/her as a political activist (his/her social self), and (s)he tries to impress the same people of his/her political activism every chance (s)he gets (his/her ideal social self). As such, his/her role identity is entrenched in the political world. Because of his/her identity being entrenched in political life, his/her time and energy are spent at the expense of other life domains such as family life, work life, and leisure life. Personality–social psychologists would characterize his/her life to be "imbalanced."

*Perfectionism* is a tendency of striving toward high personal standards and attention to what extent these standards are realized (Lo & Abbott, 2013; Slaney, Rice, Mobley, Trippi, & Ashby, 2001). Adaptive perfectionism is found when high personal standards are often perceived as attained (Slaney et al., 2001), whereas maladaptive perfectionism is found when personal standards are not seen as attained, even when objective goals are met, and attention is directed toward persistent self-criticism (Frost, Marten, Lahart, & Rosenblate, 1990). Substantial research has documented the adverse effects of maladaptive perfectionism. It is linked to depression, general distress and anxiety (Dunn, Whelton, & Sharpe, 2006; Park, Heppner, & Lee, 2010), and high strain and burnout at school (Yang & Chen, 2016) and at work (Ozbilir, Day, & Catano, 2015). This adverse effect has been explained through self-esteem (Preusser et al., 1994) and emotional dysregulation (Aldea & Rice, 2006). That is, maladaptive perfectionists tend to criticize themselves to the point of distress when they notice that the task is not completed "perfectly." Alternatively, adaptive perfectionism is related to high self-esteem (Ashby & Rice, 2002) and high engagement at work (Ozbilir et al., 2015). Adaptive perfectionists strive to reach for "perfection" in more positive and constructive ways – they do not criticize themselves when they see "imperfection" (Slaney et al., 2001).

The reader can now easily conclude that maladaptive perfectionism can lead to an imbalanced life. This dysfunctional personality characteristic motivates the person to allocate much time and energy to ensure that the task at hand is completed "perfectly." And doing so creates problems in meeting demands in other roles. For example, Jane is a maladaptive perfectionist. Because of her perfectionist proclivities, she is always running late to work because she spends too much time making sure that her kids are well situated for school. She spends too much time grooming herself to make sure she looks flawless. When at work, she spends too much time and energy on certain assigned projects to the extent she cannot complete other projects. And as such, she spends extra hours at work; she comes home habitually late. Her kids complain that they must fix dinner most evenings on their own "because mom is always late." And so on. Get the picture – the picture of a woman running ragged because of her maladaptive perfectionism.

## Organizational Factors

There are many organizational factors that may cause people to lose life balance. Examples of organizational factors include management-type positions, workplace policies that demand boundary flexibility, and supervisory nonsupportive behavior.

Let's talk about *managerial positions*. Most managerial positions are not truly 9-to-5 positions, rather they demand full-time attention – 24 hours a day and 7 days a week. This can easily lead to work exhaustion and ultimately life imbalance. Consider the study on "stress and the female retail manager" (Broadbridge, 2000, 2002). This study, conducted on male and female retail managers, found that work overload, time pressure and deadlines, staff shortages and turnover rates, and long working hours are a major source of stress, particularly among female managers. This is because female managers tend to place a higher value on family and family time than their male counterparts. Such circumstances at work interfere with family life in a big way, resulting in significant life imbalance.

Some organizations may have *workplace policies or norms that demand boundary flexibility* – management dictates that the employee is expected to use family or leisure time in situations involving deadlines and other urgent work demands. We have seen this more acutely during the COVID-19 pandemic. Managers expect their employees to deliver more and more given that many companies have forced their employees to work remotely. The underlying premise is that employees have more time to deliver because they do not spend time on commuting (e.g., Backman, 2020). In other words, the boundary flexibility strategy[1] can easily be used when the individual works at an organization that has formal policies forcing employees to use nonwork time (e.g., family time, time from leisure and social activities) to attend to work-related needs. There is some research that supports the assertion that family nonsupportive organizational policies tend to exacerbate life imbalance – employees failing to

---

[1] We already discussed boundary flexibility. This is a condition in which a person crosses over from the boundary of one life domain (e.g., work life) to another (e.g., family life); thus, spends much time and energy in the domain that has been crossed over (e.g., family), time and energy that should have been spent in the original domain (e.g., work life).

meet family and other nonwork-related needs due to these policies (e.g., Allen, 2001; Colombo, Cortese, & Ghislieri, 2013; Kossek & Distelberg, 2009; Thompson, Beauvais, & Lyness, 1999). Thus, a workplace that demands boundary flexibility should be considered a family nonsupportive organization. This means that mandating boundary flexibility is bad for many employees because it detracts from life balance, especially those who are saddled with family responsibilities.

By the same token, *supervisory nonsupportive behavior* is the most concrete form of family nonsupportive organizational policies. That is, life imbalance is exacerbated when employees perceive that their supervisor does not want to assist subordinates in managing their multiple roles at work and outside of work (Ferguson, Carlson, & Kacmar, 2015; Hammer, Kossek, Yragui, Bodner, & Hanson, 2009). Research has shown that lack of informal support of supervisors (e.g., not allowing employees to take off from work to attend to a family emergency) can be equally detracting. Specifically, supervisors who are nonsupportive of employees tend to cause employees to experience work–family conflict – disallowing their subordinates to take time off to attend to nonwork-related needs causing their subordinates to fail in meeting their essential family and other nonwork-related responsibilities (e.g., Beehr, Farmer, Glazer, Gudanowski, & Nair, 2003; Kossek, Pichler, Bodner, & Hammer, 2011).

## Societal Factors

A major study on work–family conflict was conducted by Spector et al. (2005) and involved 18 countries around the world. Taiwan, Hong Kong, and Portugal reported the highest work–family conflict, whereas Australia, the United Kingdom, and Ukraine reported the lowest. In another study comparing eight European countries (Simon, Kimmerling & Hasselhorn, 2004), work interference with family conflict was found to be greater than family interference with work conflict in all countries. Note the difference between the two types of work–family conflict, namely, "work interference with family" (WFC) versus "family interference with work" (WIF). These are two different types of work–family conflict. The former deals with conflict originating from work demand that interferes from meeting family demand, the latter is the opposite – family demand interfering with work demand. Interestingly, work interference with a family experienced by men was greater than that experienced by women in Italy. The reverse pattern was noted in the Netherlands. In yet another study comparing the United States and China, Yang et al. (2000) reported that men in China experienced higher levels of work interference with family than women in the same country. The data also indicated no gender differences in the United States.

Professor Zeynep Aycan explained that the reason for the noted cross-cultural variations may involve differences in demands and supports in work and family domains across cultural lines – differences in the number of work hours, availability of support mechanisms, and organizational work-life balance policies vary from country to country (Aycan, 2008). However, in general, she asserts that work interference with family is likely to be experienced more in countries that are going through a rapid economic transition (countries that are developing rapidly such as China and India), compared to countries with a less rapid transition (many of the sub-Saharan countries). As such, work interference with family is likely to be greater in transitioning economies (e.g., China and India), especially those with traditional gender roles, than that in the economically developed countries with egalitarian gender roles (e.g., the Scandinavian countries) (see Figure 2.1).

Pandemics, such as COVID-19, is another societal factor that has contributed significantly to life imbalance, especially for primary caregivers – meaning predominately women. For example, the American Bar Association has reported that the pandemic has disproportionately disrupted work-life balance for female lawyers in the United States (Cooper, 2020). COVID-19 has forced female lawyers to work remotely, while their children have also been forced to attend school remotely from home. As such, this outcome has turned out to be a huge burden on female lawyers. They have encountered daunting issues because of the pandemic, mostly from additional caregiving responsibilities because of gendered expectations.

The pandemic has forced more women than men to drop out of the workforce when schools went into lockdown. Women around the world have had to step back from their career in order to take care of their families. COVID-19 has disrupted workplace advancement for women, taking a huge toll on the painstaking progress that women have achieved toward professional gender equality.

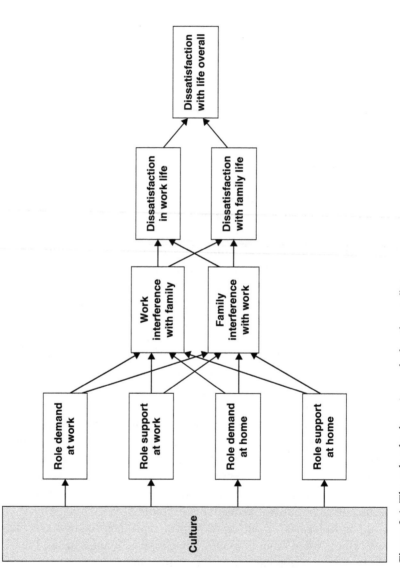

Figure 2.1 The role of culture in work–family conflict

## Summary and Conclusion

In this chapter, I provided examples of factors that cause people to lose balance in life. I broke down these factors into four categories, namely, situational, personal, organizational, and societal factors. Situational factors that cause us to lose balance are life events that occur due to a particular situation. The most obvious example of a situational factor that creates an imbalance is when an individual uses resources in one life domain at the expense of other life domains – resources that are equally needed in the other domains. As such, resource depletion in the other domains eventually creates undue hardship causing a dip in life satisfaction.

There are many personal factors that may cause us to lose balance in life. I provided three examples of personal factors, namely, priority ideology, role identity, and maladaptive perfectionism. Both priority ideology and role identity are highly interrelated. People lose balance mostly because they have a belief system that treats certain roles as exceedingly more important than others. This is an ideology priority. Their ideology priorities get them in trouble because placing a greater priority on one role comes at the expense of other roles. For example, assigning greater value to the work role ultimately leads to situations in which the individual usurps time and energy from other roles to meet demand in the priority role – in this case, work. Doing so creates a situation in which the individual fails to meet demand in nonpriority roles. The same can be said about role identity. People define themselves in terms of roles. As such, when a certain role becomes highly salient in the way the individual characterizes their identity, resources are inevitably channeled to the role identity that is highly salient. By doing so, resources are depleted from those other roles that are not salient to one's identity.

Perfectionism is yet another personal factor that usually plays an important role in creating life imbalance. A distinction was made between adaptive and maladaptive perfectionism. People who are high on maladaptive perfectionism tend to judge the performance of assigned tasks more harshly using high standards than those who are perfectionists yet adaptive. Maladaptive perfectionists often criticize themselves when they perceive that they failed to do their job "perfectly." This tendency to be highly critical of oneself drives the individual to allocate much more time and energy to those roles, time, and energy needed to meet role demand in other life domains. That is, devoting extra time and energy to those roles depletes time and energy from other important roles, which in turn causes imbalance.

Imbalance can also occur because of norms, policies, and practices within the professional organization. Life imbalance occurs frequently for individuals in managerial positions, those working in organizations that have workplace policies or norms that demand boundary flexibility, and those with nonsupportive supervisors.

With respect to societal factors, research has shown that life imbalance occurs at a high frequency in transitioning economies (e.g., China and India) where work-to-family conflict is likely to be high. This situation is particularly acute in countries with traditional gender roles, compared to the economically developed countries with egalitarian gender roles (e.g., Scandinavian countries). We also discussed how pandemics, such as COVID-19, have contributed to life imbalance, particularly for primary caregivers who are often women. Women are more frequently expected to take care of children who have been forced to be schooled remotely from home. As such, caretaking responsibilities created a huge rift in work-life balance for working women with small children.

# PART II

# Interdomain Strategies to Increase Overall Life Satisfaction and Achieve Balance

As previously mentioned, I will discuss three behavioral strategies people use to achieve life balance by prompting greater participation of satisfied life domains to contribute to life satisfaction. These are: (1) engagement in social roles in multiple life domains (explained by the principle of satisfaction limits), (2) engagement in roles in health, safety, economic, social, work, leisure, and cultural domains (explained by the principle of satisfaction of the full spectrum of human development needs), and (3) engagement in new social roles (explained by the principle of diminishing satisfaction). See Figure P2.1.

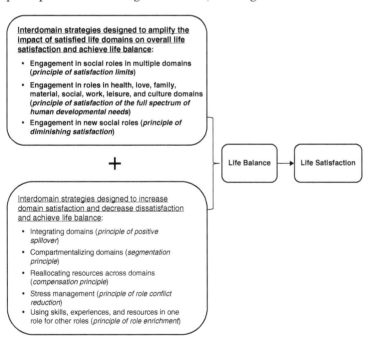

**Figure P2.1** Interdomain strategies designed to amplify the impact of satisfied life domains on overall life satisfaction and achieve balance

Specifically, Part II focuses on interdomain strategies people use to increase overall life satisfaction and achieve balance. This part contains three chapters. Chapter 3 describes the principle of satisfaction limits and how people engage in social roles in multiple domains to achieve balance. Chapter 4 describes the principle of satisfaction of the full spectrum of human developmental needs and how people engage in role in health, love, family, material, social, work, leisure, and culture domains to achieve balance. Chapter 5 describes the principle of diminishing satisfaction and how people engage in new social roles to achieve balance. The gist of these three chapters is captured in Figure P2.1 – the text highlighted in bold.

# 3 | *Engagement in Social Roles in Multiple Life Domains*

Much research has shown that engagement in social roles in work life and nonwork life (family, leisure, social, community, etc.) serves to produce a positive, fulfilling, state of mind characterized as vigor, dedication, and absorption (Schaufeli et al., 2002). *Vigor* reflects a high level of energy and mental resilience in role engagement in multiple domains. *Dedication* refers to being strongly involved in one's roles at both work and nonwork by experiencing a sense of significance, enthusiasm, and challenge. *Absorption* is characterized by being fully concentrated and happily engrossed in tasks associated with the various roles across life domains (Schaufeli & Bakker, 2004).

Individuals are likely to achieve a high level of satisfaction in life overall when they are fully engaged in multiple roles in both work life *and* nonwork life. Increasing satisfaction in multiple domains ultimately serves to increase life satisfaction at large. The effect of role engagement in social roles in multiple domains on life satisfaction can be explained through the *principle of satisfaction limits*, which we now turn to. See Figure 3.1.

The bottom-up spillover model of life satisfaction (Andrews & Withey, 1976; Campbell, Converse, & Rodgers, 1976) proposes that life satisfaction is determined by cumulative satisfaction experienced in important life domains such as satisfaction in work life, family life, social life, leisure life, spiritual life, and community life. Mathematically speaking, the compensatory model states that the life satisfaction score of an individual can be predicted by adding all of the satisfaction scores of salient life domains. For example, if one uses an 11-point satisfaction scale (−5 = high dissatisfaction to +5 = high satisfaction), then an individual (A) registering moderate satisfaction in work life (e.g., "+3"), family life (e.g., "+3"), leisure life (e.g., "+3"), social life (e.g., "+3"), and material life (e.g., "+3") should have a higher overall life satisfaction score than another individual (B) who registers high satisfaction in work life (e.g., "+5"), but no satisfaction

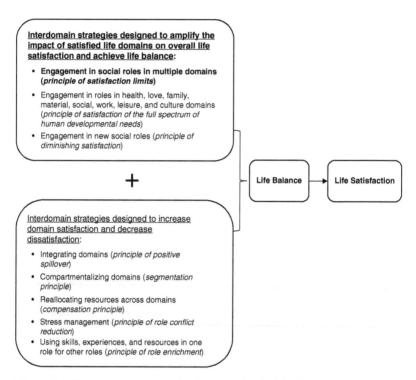

**Figure 3.1** Engagement in social roles in multiple life domains (principle of satisfaction limits) to achieve balance

across family life (e.g., "0"), leisure life (e.g., "0"), social life (e.g., "0"), and material life (e.g., "0"). This is due to the fact that the first individual (A) has a total domain satisfaction score of "15" [(+3) + (+3) + (+3) + (+3) + (+3)], whereas the latter has a total domain satisfaction score of only "+5" [(+5) + (0) + (0) + (0) + (0)]. Of course, this predictive equation assumes that work life, family life, leisure life, social life, and material life are all equally salient to both individuals. Overall life satisfaction in a given situation is accrued additively from satisfaction in multiple life domains. It should be noted that as life domain salience can vary widely from person to person based on factors such as priority ideology and role identity (as discussed in Chapter 2), this is not a perfect method for predicting life satisfaction but still a useful tool. Nevertheless, research has demonstrated that the addition of satisfaction scores from a variety of life domains is a good predictor of overall life satisfaction, and as such, we can say that there is some validity to this compensatory model of life satisfaction (e.g., Hsieh, 2003; Rojas, 2006; also see reviews by Diener, 1984; Diener et al., 1999).

## The Principle of Satisfaction Limits

The *principle of satisfaction limits* (Sirgy & Wu, 2009) posits that the amount of contribution of domain satisfaction from a single life domain to overall life satisfaction is limited. In the example of the compensatory model described above, the limit is +5 satisfaction units in each domain (scale = +5 to –5). In other words, one can achieve only a limited amount of overall satisfaction from a single life domain (a maximum of 5 satisfaction units). Using the example above, person A is satisfied in work life ("+3"), leisure life ("+3"), social life ("+3"), material life ("+3"), and family life ("+3"). His total life satisfaction (15 units) is based on a moderate degree of satisfaction in five salient life domains. Person B is satisfied with work life (+5) only. (S)he is not satisfied in family life ("0"), leisure life ("0"), social life ("0"), as well as material life ("0"). His life satisfaction score (5 units) is only impacted by the satisfaction from 1 out of 5 salient domains. In sum, an individual who is moderately satisfied in *multiple domains* is likely to experience higher life satisfaction compared to an individual who is highly satisfied in a single domain. As such, role engagement in multiple life domains produces an additive effect on overall life satisfaction (e.g., Andrews & Withey, 1976; Campbell, Converse, & Rodgers, 1976; Eakman, 2016; Hsieh, 2003; Rojas, 2006; Sirgy & Lee, 2016; Sirgy & Wu, 2009). This means that high role engagement in a single life domain with little or no role engagement in other life domains cannot contribute much to overall life satisfaction compared to high role engagement in multiple domains. This tenet counters the folklore about finding that one passion in your life and the advice to harness that passion fully. Of course, doing so may help boost personal happiness, but doing so exclusively at the expense of not engaging in other life domains may be detrimental to personal happiness.

Consider the following study: Bhargava (1995) asked study participants to discuss the life satisfaction of others (friends, family members, associates, etc.). Most participants intuitively inferred life satisfaction of others as a direct function of their satisfaction in *multiple* domains. They calculated happiness by summing satisfaction across several important domains – the more positive affect in multiple domains, the greater the subjective wellbeing (i.e., overall life satisfaction). In a work context, individuals engaging in various social roles in nonwork life domains, in addition to roles in work life, are likely to experience a high level of life satisfaction compared to those who are highly engaged only in work life (e.g., Greenhaus & Powell, 2006; Rice et al., 1985).

To reiterate, individuals who have a high level of role engagement in multiple life domains are likely to increase life balance and experience higher life satisfaction than those who have a high level of role engagement in a single domain. This effect is largely due to the principle of satisfaction limits, or the idea that there is only so much satisfaction that one can extract from a life domain to contribute to overall life satisfaction. In other words, there is a ceiling effect – a threshold above which further satisfaction cannot add value to life satisfaction overall. Compared to individuals who are engaged in a single domain, individuals who are highly engaged in multiple life domains are likely to experience higher total life satisfaction, as each individual domain cumulatively adds to that total. Those who are engaged in a single domain can produce only a limited amount of domain satisfaction (less than those who are engaged in multiple domains) that spills over to total life satisfaction. When compared to role engagement in multiple domains, role engagement in a single domain is likely to be wholly insufficient to contribute significantly to total life satisfaction.

## Strategies of Social Roles in Multiple Domains

In this section, I will describe three key strategies that well-balanced people use to engage in social roles in multiple domains. These are: (1) avoid putting all your eggs in one basket, (2) contemplate the ideal life, and (3) assess how much time you spend in what role and reallocate time. See Table 3.1.

### Avoid Putting All Your Eggs in One Basket!

"Putting all your eggs in one basket" is not a good idea. It is usually always better to have multiple baskets. Imagine if you dropped your one and only basket. All your eggs are now broken, gone, spoiled, and destroyed. If you had divided your eggs into multiple baskets, you could have spared yourself this disaster. Let's translate this adage into human terms. Mike is a detective in a law enforcement agency. He is a workaholic and is married to his job. As such, he doesn't have a

Table 3.1 *Strategies of social roles in multiple domains*

| Strategy | Description |
| --- | --- |
| Putting all your eggs in one basket | Invest time, energy, and other resources in social roles in multiple domains to guard against possible severe and catastrophic life events that may cause clinical depression or significant life dissatisfaction. |
| Imagine the ideal life | Examine life goals and aspirations, at least in the next few years. Doing so should help assess the degree of importance of the different life domains. The selected life goals should then be the basis for envisioning multiple roles and activities that must be enacted to achieve those goals. |
| Reallocate time | Examine how much time is allotted in different life domains in relation to what roles. Change allotted time in various life domains to achieve some degree of parity among the domains. |

family, he doesn't have friends to speak of, and he doesn't have hobbies. However, he loves his work. It gives him a chance to demonstrate to others both how smart he is and how essential he is in solving important criminal cases. Mike feels that his job gives him significant life satisfaction and is a major source of his personal happiness. Catastrophe strikes; he loses his job because of a political situation at work that was out of his control. After being fired, Mike has no other areas of his life upon which to draw comfort or happiness. Now compare this situation with another detective. His name is Sam. Sam is not a workaholic. He has a robust life outside of his professional career. He has a loving family – a devoted wife and two children who consider him their hero. He has good friends and neighbors. Finally, he has a hobby that he greatly enjoys, namely, aerial photography. He and his family spend much of their leisure time flying his drone and enjoying the beautiful landscape photos that the drone takes at various attraction sites. Sam is much more likely to weather the storm of being unemployed than Mike. Sam's personal happiness is likely to decrease somewhat and may cause a small degree of mental anguish, but nothing compared to Mike. Mike is likely to plummet into depression.

Upon self-evaluation, if your own situation or worst-case scenario is comparable to Mike's, then it is time to reassess your life course.

You need to make changes in your life to become engaged in multiple roles – roles that will give you some degree of satisfaction. As I demonstrated with the principle of satisfaction limits, don't rely on getting too much of your life satisfaction from a single domain. Everyone must have a well-rounded life, and this means getting involved in multiple domains. Become engaged in multiple roles, the type of roles that may result in some satisfaction. Don't expect ecstasy from any given role. A little satisfaction from a multiplicity of roles is good enough to guard against future disasters.

## Imagine the Ideal Life

Take a minute or two to imagine your ideal life. What do you want from life or what are your aspirations? Let's revisit Mike's life scenario. To reiterate, Mike is a detective who loves his job – he is a workaholic who has not found time for either family or friends. Both his priority ideology and role identity are heavily reliant upon his job, as he derives much of his self-worth from the prestige that solving criminal cases gives him. Mike's job is virtually his only source of life satisfaction and happiness.

Again, compare your situation to Mike's in order to identify certain roles and domains that you may want to invest in – roles that may give you more satisfaction – thus contributing to your overall life satisfaction. Comparing your life with Mike's should make you aware that you need to be involved "with life" – multiple roles in several domains so that you can gain additional satisfaction that will add to your overall personal happiness.

You can do this with the aid of the pie chart shown in Figure 3.2. The pie chart allows you to have a visual representation of your life domains. The chart shows several life domains: work life, family life, love life, financial life, and health and safety. These life domains are the most common domains for both men and women. Each domain is represented by a slice of the pie. You can develop your own pie chart that contains unique domains to represent your salient life domains. In other words, you may want to relabel the slices and perhaps add or delete others. But let's use the pie chart we see in Figure 3.2 as a hypothetical example to help illustrate the concept. Imagine an individual by the name of Sandra, who is a young single woman starting her first job. Examining Figure 3.2, the relative size of each slice of her pie shows that all of her domains are equally important to her at this time in her life.

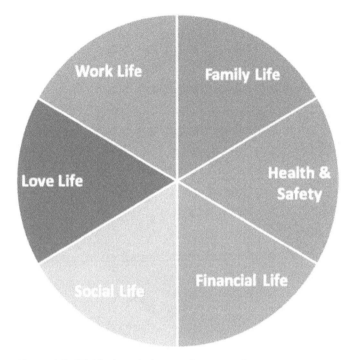

**Figure 3.2** Which domain is more important?

However, jumping forward many years, Sandra is now a 35-year-old single mom who has been divorced for the last three years. She currently has one five-year-old daughter. However, she knows that she wants to have more children and is conscious of her age and the possible risks as she gets older. In her case, she now feels that family life must take precedence over her other life domains. As such, Sandra's life goals and aspirations have changed to focus more on family life, at least for the short-term future – over the next four to five years. Looking at Figure 3.3, she has expanded the size of the family "slice" and shrunk the size of the other slices to accommodate this shift in priorities.

Once this is done, Sandra should articulate concrete roles that would allow her to achieve her new goal of having more children. In other words, what specific roles can she envision and specifically what activities she should engage in to meet role expectations in order to achieve the goal of having more children. These new roles and activities may involve putting more emphasis on her love life in order to find a potential father or investing more heavily in her health and safety domain in order to explore alternative means of conception. This plan may also mean

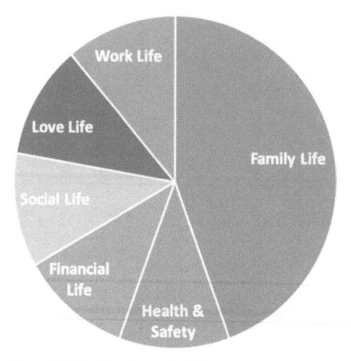

**Figure 3.3** Prioritizing the family life domain

making changes in several other domains, such as her work life and her financial life. Specifically, she makes a plan to reduce her workload and to save more money to ensure the financial stability of her future family. While Sandra has realigned her priorities to focus more on family, in order to maintain her previous overall level of life satisfaction, she should also stay minimal to moderately engaged in all of her other pie slices. In the events that her attempts to have more children failed, she would then not be as likely to experience severe emotional distress.

*Reallocate Time*

Pause for a moment and examine how you are allocating time for different roles in different life domains. Consider the case of Tom. When questioned about how many hours he spends per week to take care of work demands, he responds "around 70 hours." When asked how many hours a day he spends with his wife and children, he responds "2 hours around dinner time." When asked how many hours he spends socializing with friends, he responds "2–3 hours every month." Here, we have a person who is highly engaged with his work role but not very engaged in other life roles. Guided by the principle of satisfaction limits, the advice I would give to Tom is to reallocate the time he spends between doing work, taking care of family, and socializing with friends. He certainly needs to spend less time doing work and reallocate those hours into more time taking care of family and more time socializing with friends.

I recommend the use of the same pie chart shown in Figure 3.2 to assess the time allotted in various life domains versus the time needed to make changes in one's life to become more engaged in multiple roles in multiple domains. It should be noted that a larger emphasis on the family slice seemed to be a good thing in Sandra's case because it was part of a predetermined plan to achieve increased future life satisfaction, and once her goal is achieved, she would reallocate time to equalize her pie slices. Whereas in Tom's case, his priorities needed to be reallocated because they were significantly out of balance due to his own negligence and were causing problems in his nonwork domains.

## Conditions Favorable to Engagement in Social Roles in Multiple Domains

We will examine three sets of conditions affecting the use of this strategy (increased engagement in multiple domains) in achieving balance: situational, personal, and societal factors.

### Situational Conditions

There are many situations that call for engagement in multiple roles. An example is working in an organization that has *supportive organizational policies* and possibly a supervisor who is equally supportive. Some organizations may have workplace policies or norms that encourage employees to "have a life" outside of work – policies supporting nonwork roles outside of the organization. There are policies related to telecommuting, flex time, sick leave, disability, childcare, elderly care, health and fitness, maternity leave, paternity leave, etc. Many of these policies are designed to support nonwork roles outside of the organization (Beauregard & Henry, 2009).

Furthermore, multiple roles are more easily adopted by employees with supportive supervisors – those who want to assist subordinates in

Table 3.2 *Conditions favorable to strategies related to engagement in social roles in multiple domains*

| Condition category | Definition |
| --- | --- |
| Situational conditions | Organizational policies supportive of work-life balance; supervisors who are supportive of their employees allowing them to take time off work to attend to nonwork matters |
| Personal conditions | Nonbinary individuals (i.e., nonbinary individuals are more likely to adapt to multiple roles and experience greater life balance, much more so than either those identified as masculine or feminine) |
| Societal conditions | Countries with national policies supportive of work-life balance |

managing their multiple roles at work and outside of work (Ferguson, Carlson, & Kacmar, 2015; Hammer, Kossek, Yragui, Bodner, & Hanson, 2009).

## Personal Conditions

There are many personal characteristics that may incentivize engagement in multiple roles. One such example is individuals who identify as *gender nonbinary*. Gender nonbinary is defined as a form of gender identity – along with the traditional "masculine" and "feminine" titles – in which a person identifies as neither a male nor female but embraces aspects of both genders. A gender nonbinary individual feels comfortable in roles traditionally viewed as masculine and feminine. Traditional gender roles – societal expectations about what is considered appropriate behavior for each gender – have enforced the differentiation of many characteristics along the feminine and masculine gender divide. Nonbinary individuals can possess characteristics that have been traditionally associated with both female and male gender roles. As such, nonbinary individuals (historically referred to as androgynous) have access to a wider array of psychological competencies such as emotional regulation and situational adaptability (Cook, 1985; Sargent, 1981).

Consider the following study conducted by Swan (2016). This study examined the relationship between gender identity and job satisfaction among 100 police officers with the female gender assigned at birth but who, at the time of the study, identified with the masculine gender identity. The study found that these police officers experienced less job satisfaction than those who identified as gender nonbinary (or androgynous). Another study (Wierda-Boer, Gerris, & Vermulst, 2008) surveying Dutch dual-earner couples with young children examined how adaptive strategies and gender ideology related to work-life balance. The study found that traits traditionally linked with the opposite sex (i.e., masculine traits for women and feminine traits for men) were beneficial in enhancing work-life balance for both sexes. As such, the research is highly suggestive of the fact that nongender conforming individuals are more likely to adapt to multiple roles and experience greater life balance, much more so than either those who identify as either masculine or feminine.

## Societal Conditions

At the macrolevel, there are also many conditions that favor engagement in multiple roles. One prime example is *supportive national policies*. Many countries have different welfare state regimes in which work-life balance support varies. Even within Europe, research has shown significant differences among countries in their support for work-life balance policies (Den Dulk & Van Doorne-Huiskes, 2007; OECD, 2001, 2007). The most extensive national work-life policies are in Scandinavian countries. The Scandinavian countries have been able to develop and implement far-reaching and encompassing work-life balance policies, such as parental leave, early childhood education, and childcare. For example, Sweden has been lauded as the first country to introduce parental leave for both mothers and fathers to take time off work to care for their children.

As such, I can comfortably suggest that the multiple role strategy of work-life balance can easily be implemented in countries where there are existing formal policies supporting practices related to work-life balance.

## Summary and Conclusion

This chapter focused on the notion that life balance can be achieved, at least partly, through engagement in social roles in work and nonwork domains. Doing so contributes significantly to a high level of satisfaction in life overall. The reason for this is explained using the principle of satisfaction limits, which posits that the contribution of domain satisfaction from a single life domain to overall life satisfaction is limited. In other words, high role engagement in a single life domain with little or no role engagement in other life domains cannot match total life satisfaction compared to moderate role engagement in multiple domains. Of course, the more an individual is engaged in certain social roles, the happier they become with these roles and associated life domains, which in turn contributes to overall life satisfaction.

I then described three key strategies that well-balanced people use to engage in social roles in multiple domains, namely (1) avoid putting all your eggs in one basket, (2) contemplate the ideal life, and (3) assess how much time you spend in what role and reallocate time. "Avoid putting all your eggs in one basket" is a personal strategy that calls for investment of time, energy, and other resources in social roles in multiple domains to guard against possible severe and catastrophic life events that may cause clinical depression or significant life dissatisfaction. The "imagine the ideal life" strategy calls for the individual to examine one's life goals and aspirations on the near horizon. Doing so should help assess the degree of importance of different life domains. The selected life goals should then be the basis for envisioning multiple roles and activities that must be enacted to achieve those goals. Last but not least is the "re-allocate time" strategy. This strategy calls for examining how much time is allotted in different life domains in relation to what roles. The individual should change the allotted time in various life domains to achieve some degree of parity among the domains.

Then, I concluded the chapter by describing three sets of conditions affecting the use of the aforementioned strategies: situational, personal, and societal factors. Organizational policies supportive of work-life balance is an example of a favorable situational condition. Another favorable situational condition involves supervisors who are supportive of their employees, by allowing them to take time off work to attend to nonwork matters for example. With respect to personal conditions favorable to the multiple domains strategy, I identified gender nonbinary individuals. Individuals whose gender identity is nonbinary are more likely to adapt to multiple roles and experience greater life balance – much more so than those who identify as masculine or feminine. Finally, I made the case that countries with national policies supportive of work-life balance are an example of a societal condition favorable to the multiple domain strategy.

# 4 | Engagement in Roles in Health, Love, Family, Material, Social, Work, Leisure, and Culture Domains

In Chapter 3, I made the case that people should optimize their life satisfaction (enhance their life satisfaction to an acceptable level) by actively engaging in social roles in multiple domains. The question that arises based on the preceding argument is "which domains?" Life satisfaction is significantly increased when the individual engages in roles in life domains that can satisfy the *full spectrum of human development needs* (Maslow, 1970). As such, life balance can be best achieved through active engagement in social roles in multiple domains that serve to also satisfy both basic and growth needs (basic needs are considered survival-related needs such as the need for food and shelter, while growth needs are related to higher-order needs such as social needs and needs related to esteem, self-actualization, knowledge, and creativity). Specifically, engagement in social roles in health, love, family, and material domains serves to satisfy mostly basic needs. By contrast, engagement in social roles in social, work, leisure, and culture domains serves to satisfy growth needs. Let us be more specific.

Sirgy and Wu (2009) have argued that subjective wellbeing is not simply cumulative positive minus negative affect – irrespective of the source (the specific needs related to the experienced affect). Subjective wellbeing or overall life satisfaction involves the satisfaction on the full spectrum of human developmental needs – the full range of needs, not a handful of arbitrarily selected needs. In other words, one cannot substitute positive affect related to one need with another need. To illustrate this point, let us consider the following example. There are two individuals, person A and person B. Person A has "+2" satisfaction units (on a scale varying from –5 to mean strong dissatisfaction to +5 meaning strong satisfaction) in each of the following domains related to basic needs: health life, love life, family life, and material life. In other words, person A is satisfied in domains related to his/her basic needs, with a total score of "+8" satisfaction units [(+2) + (+2) + (+2) + (+2)].

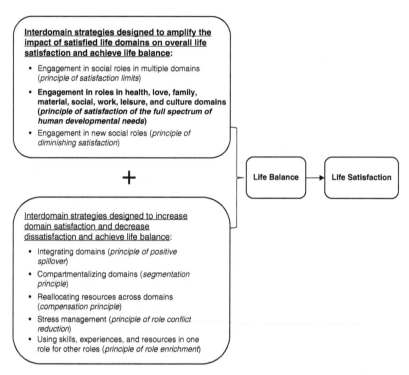

**Figure 4.1** Engagement in roles in health, love, family, material, social, work, leisure, and culture domains (principle of satisfaction of the full spectrum of human developmental needs) to achieve balance

Person A is similarly satisfied in life domains related to growth needs (social life, work life, leisure life, and cultural life) with another total of "+8" [(+2) + (+2) + (+2) + (+2)]. Summing up person A's domain satisfaction scores, we obtain a total amount of "16" units of domain satisfaction (+8 satisfaction units from domains related to basic needs and another +8 satisfaction units from domains related to growth needs). Now let us compare this case with person B who is highly satisfied with basic needs only. Person B is highly satisfied in all domains related to his basic needs, with a total score of "+20" satisfaction units [(+5) + (+5) + (+5) + (+5)], while they are dissatisfied in domains related to his growth needs, a total of "−8" satisfaction units [(−2) + (−2) + (−2) + (−2)]. As such, the total domain satisfaction score for person B is also "+12." However, person A is likely to report a higher degree of life satisfaction than person B because person A has *balanced satisfaction* from life domains related to *both basic and growth needs*, whereas person B has unbalanced domain satisfaction (high satisfaction in domains related to basic needs but low satisfaction in domains related to growth needs). See Figure 4.1.

## The Principle of Satisfaction of the Full Spectrum of Human Developmental Needs

Let us delve deeper to understand the psychology underlying the concept of balanced satisfaction. We will do so by discussing the *principle of satisfaction of the full spectrum of human developmental needs*. This principle posits that individuals who are satisfied with the full spectrum of developmental needs (i.e., satisfaction of growth needs as well as basic needs) are likely to have a high level of life satisfaction relative to those who are less satisfied (e.g., Alderfer, 1972; Herzberg, 1966; Maslow, 1970; Matuska, 2012; Sheldon, Cummins, & Kamble, 2010; Sheldon & Niemiec, 2006). Of course, you say. However, the point is not satisfaction *per se* but the source of the satisfaction, and in this instance, the *full spectrum of human developmental needs* (i.e., basic and growth needs). In other words, higher levels of need satisfaction contribute to higher levels of life satisfaction if and when the source of satisfaction stems from both basic and growth needs, not basic needs alone and not growth needs alone. When people engage in multiple roles across life domains, they are likely to obtain access to more psychological and physical resources, which in turn increases opportunities for the satisfaction of many basic and growth needs. Seeking to satisfy a specific need in a single life domain does not positively contribute much to life satisfaction (Sirgy et al., 1995). That is, when people engage in multiple roles, they are likely to experience the satisfaction of growth needs (i.e., social, knowledge, aesthetics, self-actualization, and self-transcendence needs) as well as the satisfaction of basic needs (i.e., health, safety, and economic needs). Satisfaction of both sets of basic and growth needs contributes significantly and positively to life satisfaction.

Specifically, Sirgy and Wu (2009) have described how people conduct their lives in order to fulfill their developmental needs. In order to satisfy developmental needs, individuals engage in a variety of activities toward that purpose. The events related to those activities and their outcomes generate a certain amount of satisfaction and dissatisfaction.

These affective reactions are organized and stored in memory in certain life domains such as health, love, family, and economic. For example, in order to satisfy their biological and health-related needs, people engage in a variety of activities such as eating right, exercising regularly, getting regular checkups, and so on. When a man is then asked how he feels about his health life, he is likely to reflect on his affective experiences in relation to those health-related activities. When the same person is asked about his love life, he might reflect on his affective experiences related to love, romantic relationships, and sex. When asked about his family life, he might reflect on those experiences related to his spouse and children, his residence, his neighborhood, and his community. Financial issues and experiences related to money, income, standard of living, and material possessions are likely to be segmented in material life and mostly related to basic needs. With respect to growth needs (e.g., social, esteem, self-actualization, self-transcendence, aesthetics, and knowledge needs), experiences may be segmented in life domains such as social life, work life, leisure life, and cultural life. However, this is not to say that a variety of developmental needs can be met in a single domain. Consider the work domain, for example. Through work life, both basic (i.e., economic, health and safety, and family-related needs) and growth needs (i.e., social, esteem, self-actualization, self-transcendence, knowledge, and aesthetic needs) can be met. To reiterate, in every life domain, a variety of developmental needs can be met. However, certain life domains are predisposed to meet certain developmental needs more so than others. As such, we argue that health, love, family, and economic domains are likely to reflect satisfaction resulting more from meeting basic needs than growth needs. Conversely, social life, work life, leisure life, and cultural life are domains likely to reflect satisfaction resulting more from meeting growth than basic needs.

Support for this principle (the principle of satisfaction of the full spectrum of human developmental needs) comes from a body of evidence showing that materialism is negatively correlated with life satisfaction (see Wright and Larsen, 1993, for a meta-analysis of the research findings). Specifically, materialistic people can be viewed as imbalanced in that they pursue wealth and material possessions to the exclusion of other important goals in life. Materialistic people who are able to hoard material wealth may feel successful and happy with their material life. However, placing undue emphasis on making money (to satisfy basic needs such as biological and safety needs) is likely to lead them to neglect other growth needs such as social, esteem, self-actualization, self-transcendence, aesthetics, and knowledge needs. It is no wonder that many studies have shown that materialism is negatively correlated with life satisfaction. In essence, materialism is an "excessive" condition that adversely impacts life balance because it disallows the materialistic individual from satisfying a full range of human developmental needs in multiple life domains. "Workaholism" is also an excessive condition with similar effects on life balance and subjective wellbeing. A workaholic constantly seeks professional success to the exclusion of other important life goals. The generic case here is that individuals who fixate on a specific domain or role are likely to suffer from life dissatisfaction because they are forgoing the satisfaction of the full spectrum of human developmental needs, both basic and growth needs.

Furthermore, as previously discussed, Matuska (2012) conceptualized life balance as congruence among both desired and actual time spent in activities and equivalence in the degree of discrepancy between desired and actual time spent across *activities that satisfy basic and growth needs* (needs related to health, relationship, challenge/interest, and identity). The author conducted a study that successfully demonstrated a strong association between life balance and personal wellbeing.

In sum, the preceding discussion can be captured as follows: Individuals who have a high level of role engagement in life domains related to both basic needs (e.g., health, love, family, and material/economic domains) *and* growth needs (e.g., social, work, leisure, and culture domains) are likely to experience greater satisfaction among life domains contributing to higher life satisfaction than those who have a high level of role engagement in domains related to only basic **or** growth needs. Specifically, compared to individuals who are engaged in roles only in select domains, those engaging in multiple domains satisfying both basic and growth needs are likely to experience more life satisfaction. Role engagement in health, love, family, and material (economic) domains is likely to satisfy mostly basic needs (survival needs such as having enough resources to deal with health and safety issues), whereas role engagement in social, work, leisure, and culture is likely to satisfy mostly growth needs (higher-order needs such as social, esteem, self-actualization, aesthetics, and knowledge).

The combined and balanced effects of satisfaction of both basic and growth needs serve to increase life satisfaction. That is, satisfaction of the full spectrum of human developmental needs (balance between basic and growth need satisfaction) produce the highest level of life satisfaction.

## Strategies of Engagement in Roles in Health, Love, Family, Material (Economic), Social, Work, Leisure, and Culture Domains

This section discusses several basic strategies designed to meet basic needs. I refer to them as "maintenance strategies" because these are a means to help us continue "functioning." We need to function on a daily basis, and yes, we need to function reasonably well to be able to flourish. We will address "flourishing strategies" in the next section.

At one time, I had a colleague at my university who had an imbalanced life. He devoted more than 90 percent of his work time to research and writing – specifically research and writing designed to produce a publication. Being at a research university, research and writing is a must. We live by the adage: "publish or perish." However, in reality, it is "publish and prosper." My colleague was highly motivated to engage in this endeavor because it satisfied his "growth needs" – the need for esteem, self-actualization, knowledge, and creativity. The problem was that he was so sloppy. His office was a mess. He would have a hard time finding reports, books, and research materials in his office. Luckily, he had at least two graduate assistants and a secretary who helped. Thus, maintenance tasks (such as organizing files, developing PowerPoint slides, typing reports and manuscripts, making travel arrangements, servicing his computer, and other multimedia gadgets) were someone else's responsibility, never his. Even his contact list on his phone was not his responsibility. Unfortunately, modern technology has displaced graduate assistants and secretaries. In the modern landscape of today's universities, graduate assistants are not often assigned "gofer-like duties." University administration expects faculty to involve their graduate students with their own research leading to publications. That is, graduate students become, in essence, research interns working on research projects that eventually lead to publication, where they are acknowledged for their research input, if their career goals involve academics. Alternatively, the research effort should pave the way to a professional position in the industry. Secretaries also no longer perform "secretarial duties" in the traditional, historical sense. They no longer support faculty typing their manuscripts and making travel arrangements. Their positions have transformed into technical specialties such as financial accounting, inventory and logistics, research compliance, among others.

Going back to my "old-fashioned" colleague, the "maintenance" support he once had is now no longer available. His passion for focusing on research and writing has been hampered by his own chaotic lifestyle. His scholarly productivity plummeted, and he refused to adjust to modernity in the rapidly evolving landscape of research universities. He became frustrated and angry at every turn. He complained constantly that the world around him kept crashing down. Most other university faculty learned to adjust by assuming new roles that were once relegated to graduate assistants and secretaries. They learned how to use information technology to get things done efficiently. Thus, to engage in "flourishing" activities, one also needs to do "housekeeping." Housekeeping duties are required to allow individuals to both function and flourish.

So, what are some maintenance strategies – strategies to facilitate normal functioning? Maintenance strategies tend to satisfy basic needs, not growth needs. Conversely, do flourishing strategies involve behaviors designed to satisfy growth needs? We can identify maintenance versus flourishing strategies by focusing on life domains – health, love, family, material, social, work, leisure, and culture. Here is a list of maintenance versus flourishing behaviors couched in the aforementioned domains (see Table 4.1).

## Maintenance and Flourishing Strategies in Relation to Personal Health

A major component of the personal health domain is maintaining a healthy lifestyle through physical exercise and eat a well-balanced diet. Get a physical exam annually as well as other routine medical exams. If symptoms of illness develop, consult a medical professional promptly and comply with physician orders. This is the least you can do – meaning "maintenance." By contrast, you can do much more to flourish in relation to personal health. Turn your physical exercise routine into a passion. Make it an enjoyable sport by joining a local

**Table 4.1** *Maintenance and flourishing strategies commonly used in health, love, family, material (economic), social work, leisure, and culture domains*

| Life domain | Maintenance and flourishing strategies |
| --- | --- |
| Health and safety | *Maintenance strategies*: Maintain a healthy lifestyle through physical exercise and eating a well-balanced diet. Have regular health checkups and comply with doctors' orders. <br> *Flourishing strategies*: Make physical exercise a sport. Make cooking a hobby. Plan social outings with nutritious meals and physical exercise. |
| Love life | *Maintenance strategies*: Make future plans to maintain your relationship with your romantic partner, such as buying a house together. Attend couples counseling to maintain a healthy relationship. <br> *Flourishing strategies*: Take your spouse out for a romantic dinner. Get together with good friends as a couple. Travel with your significant other. Reminisce about positive experiences you shared as a couple. Make love in exotic locations. |
| Family life | *Maintenance strategies*: Maintaining a good relationship with family members requires significant time, effort, and money. This may include childcare, schooling, meal preparation, attending to the sick, elderly care, doing household chores, and shopping for family needs, among a multitude of other "essential" tasks. <br> *Flourishing strategies*: Flourishing entails injecting fun and passion into the family mix. Examples include planning a family vacation, holding social events with family members, engaging in sports with family members, and recreating and engaging in leisure activities with family members. |
| Material (economic) life | *Maintenance strategies*: Perform a job that produces enough income to pay the bills and buy the essentials. Buying necessities such as groceries and personal care items. <br> *Flourishing strategies*: Invest for future growth and consume goods and services that have elements of novelty and excitement. |

**Table 4.1** *(cont.)*

| Life domain | Maintenance and flourishing strategies |
|---|---|
| Social life | *Maintenance strategies*: Attend important family functions such as weddings as well as funerals. Support relatives and friends when they are sick or are in need. Attend social events at work to strengthen the social bond with your coworkers.<br>*Flourishing strategies*: Play an exciting game with your friends on a regular basis. Go out with friends on a social outing – dinner and movie. Join a social club that meets regularly. |
| Work life | *Maintenance strategies*: Arrive or begin work on time every day, avoid excessive absences, and perform your required job duties in a timely manner.<br>*Flourishing strategies*: Set career goals. Develop concrete plans to attain career goals. Monitor the progress toward goal attainment. |
| Leisure life | *Maintenance strategies*: Engage in leisure activities that can help you relax and destress.<br>*Flourishing strategies*: Engage in competitive games that allow you to express related skills and mastery. Start a new hobby that you enjoy. |
| Cultural life | *Maintenance strategies*: Engage in cultural activities to learn about your own culture and the culture of other people in other places.<br>*Flourishing strategies*: Travel to destinations that reflect aspects of your own personal identity, spirituality, and heritage. Travel to destinations to learn about the cultures of other people to expand your knowledge and wisdom. |

intermural team and integrate it into your lifestyle. Participate in the sport not only because you want to stay fit but also for the fun of it. With respect to food and nutrition, take up cooking. Look up delicious and nutritious recipes and start cooking – or learn to cook. Share your healthy meals with others. Make every meal a social occasion. Go to restaurants that have healthy and nutritious food and beverages. Make these outings social and fun.

Consider the following study that my colleagues and I conducted related to physical exercise (Lee, Sirgy, Yu, & Chalamon, 2015). Our study examined how satisfaction of self-expressiveness and hedonic needs related to physical exercise, which influenced a variety of well-being outcomes (i.e., healthy eating, BMI, satisfaction with health, and subjective wellbeing). The study involved a survey of college students at universities in three countries: the United States, France, and South Korea. Examples of survey items for self-expressiveness included: "This physical activity gives me the greatest feeling of really being alive"; "When I engage in this physical activity I feel more intensely involved than I do when engaged in most other activities"; and "This physical activity gives me the strongest feeling that I am who I really am." The items for hedonic enjoyment included: "When I engage in this physical activity, I feel more satisfied than I do when I engage in most other activities" and "This physical activity gives me my strongest sense of enjoyment." The study findings indicated that self-expressiveness associated with routine and frequent physical exercise is likely to exert a strong influence on healthy eating habits. Healthy eating was also shown to be associated with other personal positive outcomes such as low body mass index, increased satisfaction with personal health, and increased subjective wellbeing.

As such, engaging in maintenance and flourishing activities in the health and safety domain is a MUST for achieving balance and building a solid foundation for personal happiness.

## Maintenance and Flourishing Strategies in Love Life

There are two strong motives that govern our love life, namely, the need to belong and desire (Kim & Hatfield, 2004). The need to belong (or "companionate love") refers to the need to have a partner in life – to belong to this partner and to feel that we belong to them. The attachment to a life partner is fundamental. It involves maintaining a stable relationship that provides a sense of security. Families are built around this need. The propagation of the species is built around this need. To satisfy this need to the fullest, you must invest resources to "maintain" your romantic relationship with your significant other. This means the investment of time, effort, and perhaps money too.

The need for desire (or "passionate love") is different. Desire involves lust, excitement, and passion. You have likely felt romantic desire at some point in your life, typically strongest in the initial stages of any type of relationship. Usually desire wanes, the feelings of lust, excitement, and passion dissipate over time. Investments of time, effort, and money are necessary to keep passionate love alive and in turn to ensure that your love life flourishes. Examples of flourishing strategies in love life include planning a date. Take your partner out for a romantic dinner. While dining, don't talk about the mundane but about exciting things such as getting together with good friends, going off on a cruise, and doing some traveling in exotic places. Talk about shared past events that you found exciting or future adventures. Take your partner to an exotic location and make love. Use your imagination to inject more excitement into the relationship.

Consider the following study conducted by Kim and Hatfield (2004). College students from the United States and South Korea participated in a survey capturing love type (companionate vs. passionate love) and various measures of subjective wellbeing. The study found that the two love types are related to subjective wellbeing in different ways. Specifically, life satisfaction was more strongly predicted by companionate love than by passionate love. By contrast, positive and negative emotions were more associated with passionate love than by companionate love. One can argue that life satisfaction is a higher form of subjective wellbeing that is more related to "flourishing" than "maintenance," whereas positive and negative affect is a lower form of subjective wellbeing and as such can be viewed as more related to "maintenance" than "flourishing" (Sirgy, 2019, 2020).

The key point here is to do both: Do your best to maintain the relationship but also do your best to keep the relationship exciting by injecting passion into it on a regular basis. Both activities in your love life are essential to achieving life balance and ensuring an acceptable level of life satisfaction.

## Maintenance and Flourishing Strategies in Family Life

Family life extends beyond the household. Family life often involves a combination of children, parents, siblings, and possibly other close relatives. Family structure tends to be different for those who are single, divorced, or widowed; as such, family members are likely to be defined differently in these households. Maintaining good relationships with family members is also very important to personal happiness. For those who are divorced, maintaining a good relationship with your ex is equally important. Maintaining a good relationship with family members requires significant time, effort, and money. This includes aspects such as childcare, schooling, meal preparation, attending to the sick, elderly care, household chores, and shopping for family needs, among a multitude of other "essential" tasks.

Flourishing in family life entails injecting excitement into the family mix. Examples include planning a family vacation (or a family reunion), holding social events with family members, engaging in sports or activities with family members, recreating and engaging in leisure activities with family members, and making meal preparation a social event where each family member is delegated a task. Use your imagination and become creative in planning other "fun" activities with family members.

Consider the following seminal study conducted by Professor Christopher Ellison (1990). Using data from the National Survey of Black Americans, the study investigated relationships between kinship bonds and subjective wellbeing. The study found that subjective family closeness is a strong predictor of personal happiness among all Black individuals, and the same construct (subjective family closeness) is a strong predictor of life satisfaction among older Black adults only. I previously argued that there is much evidence in the wellbeing literature, suggesting that personal happiness is a lower form of subjective wellbeing directly related to positive and negative affects, whereas life satisfaction is a higher form (Sirgy, 2019, 2020). Lower forms of subjective wellbeing can be construed as directly related to "maintenance" activities, whereas higher forms of subjective wellbeing are more related to "flourishing" activities. As such, the finding that subjective family closeness is a strong predictor of life satisfaction among older Black adults is not surprising given that life satisfaction is related to "flourishing" activities.

## Maintenance and Flourishing Strategies in Material (Economic) Life

Making money and spending money on material things can also be decomposed into maintenance and flourishing strategies too. Making money to pay the bills and taking care of urgent and immediate household needs are "maintenance" activities. By contrast, investing in the stock market and business ventures should be considered as "flourishing" activities. The same can be said with respect to shopping. One can shop for the bare essentials such as food, beverages, clothing, and household goods; and one can shop for items such as a fancy sports car, a sailboat, and other luxury goods. Imagine going to the shopping mall, not necessarily to buy something you need but to simply browse and experience the aesthetics and ambiance of the mall. The latter activities may be viewed as "flourishing," whereas the former activities are viewed as "maintenance."[1]

The point here is that one needs to engage in life in full. To do this in relation to material life means to produce enough income to pay the bills and buy the essentials (i.e., maintenance activities) and invest for future growth and consume goods and services that have elements of novelty and excitement. Maintenance and flourishing activities in material life are a MUST to achieve life balance.

## Maintenance and Flourishing Strategies in Social Life

We, as human beings, are social beings. However, saying that we are simply social beings is an understatement; we are "hyper social." This means that being alone and feeling lonely works against our most basic human needs. We like to be with people, interact with them, and feel connected to others. We join groups of all kinds such as professional groups, religious groups, educational groups, sports groups, recreation groups, and familial groups, among many others. Social networking is very important to "having a life." Becoming a member and maintaining that membership in social groups is built in our genetic code. There is an interesting book by Lydia Denworth (2020) that was recently published. The title is *Friendship: The evolution, biology, and extraordinary power of life's fundamental bond.* Denworth demonstrates that social connection with others has been recognized by wellbeing researchers as fundamental to public health. Creating and maintaining social bonds improves our health, both physically and mentally. Those with strong social bonds are less likely to be depressed and more likely to be happy and live longer.

An example of a maintenance element is social life may be attending important social functions such as weddings and funerals of your

---

[1] Some readers may find it difficult to differentiate between maintenance and flourishing strategies in material (economic) life. This may be due to the confounding effects of socioeconomic status. Specifically, flourishing strategies for working-class individuals are likely to be maintenance strategies for upper class individuals.

extended circle of friends and acquaintances. Offering support or gathering to comfort friends when they are sick or are in need is also a maintenance function in social life. Attending social events at work to make sure that you are viewed as an integral member of the firm is also a maintenance function.

Flourishing in social life is about passion, excitement, and fun. Playing games such as bridge, bingo, or trivia with your friends on a regular basis is a social event that allows the individual to flourish. The same can be said about planning outings with friends – from going out to dinner and movies to organizing vacations. Belonging to social clubs is also an example of a flourishing strategy, examples would include a chess club, intermural sporting team, book club, or even a yacht club.

To experience authentic satisfaction in social life and achieve life balance, one needs to engage in both maintenance and flourishing social activities.

### Maintenance and Flourishing Strategies in Work Life

Do you work to live or do you live to work? Many industrial/organizational psychologists have long asked this question and answered it with a resounding answer: BOTH. In other words, we work to make a living – to make an income that supports our way of living. We work to meet our basic needs – food security, housing and shelter, health and safety, family needs, etc. We also work because we are wired to work. Not working is against our human nature. Through work, our many growth needs – social needs, esteem needs, need for self-actualization, need for knowledge, and aesthetics and creativity needs – can be met.

This distinction is made clear when you ask yourself whether your job is just a job or a conduit to a fulfilling career. If it is just a job, then your work life is mostly about maintenance – your job allows you to maintain a lifestyle you grew accustomed to. As such, it is important that you engage in work to make a decent living, the kind of income that can support your basic needs and possibly your family needs. However, a job as a career is much more. It goes beyond maintenance. It is about flourishing. The goal of working just to make money is not likely to be fulfilling. Work, for most people who identify themselves as having a "career," provides them with the opportunity to set for themselves important lifelong goals and to strive to meet these goals. Monitoring goal progress and anticipating goal attainment are key to positive emotions related to achievement, pride, hope, optimism, esteem, meaning, purpose, self-determination, competence, autonomy, and internal locus of control. Knowing this, it is important to develop a career and work toward career development.

Much of the research literature on work motivation in industrial/organizational psychology makes a distinction between intrinsic and extrinsic motivation (Amabile, 1993), which can be viewed in terms of the traditional distinction between low-order and high-order needs (Maslow, 1962). A person who is motivated to do a job because it is a job that provides them a paycheck and other fringe benefits is "extrinsically motivated." As such, the job serves to satisfy mostly low-order (basic) rather than high-order (growth) needs. Conversely, a job considered to be part of a career involves intrinsic motivation – the job satisfies high-order (growth) needs. Low-order needs are essentially needs related to survival: biological needs (needs for food, water, air, sex, etc.), health and safety needs, social and family needs, and ultimately the minimum financial resources for the sustenance of oneself (and possibly one's family). Low-order needs are essentially basic needs (needs related to survival and the propagation of the human species). Satisfying basic needs involve "maintenance" activities in work life. By contrast, high-order needs are growth related. They include a wide assortment of needs such as social and relatedness needs; esteem and effectance (perception of agency or control of one's environment) needs; self-actualization needs; needs related to aesthetics; and creativity, intellectual, and autonomy needs, among others. Many of these human needs are met through one's career. Satisfying growth needs involve "flourishing" activities in work life.

Research (e.g., Herzberg, 1979; Sanjeev & Surya, 2016) has demonstrated that a job that fails to meet basic needs causes much job dissatisfaction (negative feelings and emotions such as anger, fear, anxiety, despair, hopelessness, and depression). However, a job that meets basic needs does not contribute much to job satisfaction or positive emotions (e.g., happiness and joy). A good job that meets basic needs can provide only relief, not joy or happiness. Conversely, a job that satisfies high-order needs can contribute significantly to positive emotions such as happiness. A job that fails to meet high-order needs is not likely to cause much job dissatisfaction.

As such, to help achieve life balance, we all need to engage in both maintenance and flourishing activities in our work life.

## Maintenance and Flourishing Strategies in Leisure Life

Consider the following example of a couple visiting a golf resort for leisure. The husband is an avid golfer, but the wife is not. The golf resort is a beautiful place with all types of amenities: spa and massage, fine dining, a shuttle service to neighboring attraction sites, a social club, and several gift shops, among others. Who is likely to experience a higher level of leisure wellbeing? The husband or the wife? The answer is the husband is likely to experience more happiness than the wife. The wife is likely to experience some positive affect playing golf and enjoying the resort amenities, but the husband is likely to experience a heightened sense of leisure wellbeing because he is an avid golfer. That is, visiting the golf resort serves mostly as a maintenance function for the wife; however, for the husband, the leisure experience is not simply about maintenance but also is a flourishing experience.

So, you see, leisure can be experienced differently. When we talk about leisure wellbeing as "maintenance," we are referring to a hedonic experience – an experience involving fun and pleasure. By contrast, leisure wellbeing as "flourishing" is more than hedonic; it is "eudaimonic" (Bosnjak et al., 2016). Eudaimonic happiness is achieved through experiences that are intrinsic, meaningful, and growth oriented. Eudaimonic happiness might be generated if the leisure activity reflects the person's identity or their experience is enduring and long-lasting. Hedonic wellbeing is much more ephemeral and momentary. It is fun, pleasurable, and exciting, but highly situational. That is, the person experiences the positive emotions in that brief span of time, then these positive feelings dissipate. For example, going on a vacation completely planned by your significant other is likely to produce hedonic happiness. By contrast, the travel planner (your significant other) is most likely to experience eudaimonic happiness.

Consider the study conducted by Kuykendall et al. (2020). The researchers compared the extent to which watching TV with other leisure activities (reading, traveling to exotic places, engaging in sports, etc.) served to enhance wellbeing. They hypothesized that compared to other leisure activities, watching TV serves to enhance wellbeing by allowing the person to relax and detach himself from daily stress. However, TV watching is less conducive to higher-order needs such as the need for meaning, mastery, and affiliation. Relaxation and detachment from stress are outcomes related to basic needs, whereas outcomes associated with meaning, mastery, and affiliation are essentially related to growth needs. They tested this hypothesis by instructing study participants to report their subjective wellbeing using a daily diary. The study results were supportive of their hypothesis. As such, TV watching seems to serve a maintenance function, whereas other more engaging leisure activities are better geared to serve a flourishing function.

In sum, to achieve life balance, we need to engage in both maintenance and flourishing activities in social life.

## Maintenance and Flourishing Strategies in Cultural Life

Cultural life is about intellectual and emotional experiences related to culture – one's own culture or the culture of others. Examples include watching a movie that has a major historical element. It is about visiting another country and experiencing its culture in terms of food and beverage, language, religion, art, and traditional customs and rituals. Cultural experiences involve a cognitive (i.e., educational or intellectual) element as well as an affective (i.e., emotional) element.

Consider the following scenario: A couple, Barbara and Sarah, visiting the National Museum of the American Indian, a major cultural icon of the history of the American Indian in the United States. Barbara is of American Indian descendent; Sarah is of Anglo descent. Visiting the museum is highly educational for both, a cultural experience par excellence. Sarah walks away from the museum feeling enriched with more knowledge about the history of the United States and the role of native Indians in the development of American culture and institutions. For Sarah, this experience was mostly a maintenance function in relation to cultural wellbeing. The experience served to educate, socialize, and inform Sarah about an important constituency of American landscape and its people. Understanding this history is a prerequisite to understanding American history, and every American is obligated to understand their history; this is part of their civic obligations. However, for Barbara, who has American Indian ancestry, this cultural experience can be characterized as "flourishing." It was not only educational in the abstract sense; the experience is much more meaningful because it is part of her own identity, who she is and where she came from. Such a visit is an important element in her emotional life.

As such, to enrich one's sense of cultural wellbeing, one has not only to engage in cultural activities that serve the maintenance function but also the flourishing function.

## Conditions Favorable to Maintenance versus Flourishing Activities

In this section, I will describe examples of conditions that favor the use of maintenance and flourishing strategies. These conditions are related to situational, personal, and societal factors. See Table 4.2.

Table 4.2 *Conditions favorable to maintenance versus flourishing activities*

| Condition category | Variables |
| --- | --- |
| Situational conditions | Situations that highlight deficits in a specific life domain call for maintenance-type activities. By contrast, nondeficit situations call for flourishing activities. |
| Personal conditions | Individuals who are prevention focused are likely to favor maintenance-type activities in various life domains, whereas those who are promotion focused are likely to favor flourishing-type activities. |
| Societal conditions | Maintenance activities take precedence over flourishing activities in adverse times. By contrast, flourishing activities are afforded in times of abundance – when things are going well in the natural, political, economic, and social environment. |

## Situational Conditions

There are many situations that warrant maintenance over flourishing activities; and conversely, other situations that may call for flourishing activities. Specifically, situations that highlight deficits in a specific life domain call for maintenance-type activities. By contrast, nondeficit situations call for flourishing activities. For example, we discussed the fact that maintaining a good relationship with family members is very important to personal happiness. Examples of important maintenance activities in family life included childcare, schooling, meal preparation, attending to the sick, elderly care, household chores, and shopping for family needs, among other tasks. Any situation that highlights a deficit in relation to these maintenance activities requires mending. That is, if the deficit is in childcare, then you need to do whatever it takes to improve. If your kids are failing at school, then you need to assist them in the best way you can – hiring tutors, spending more time helping with homework, and providing a better home environment – to change the situation.

Flourishing strategies should be implemented in nondeficit situations. We mentioned examples such as planning a family vacation or a family reunion, holding social events with family members, engaging in sports with family members, and making a meal a social event, among other "fun" activities. Consider the latter example, namely, "turning meal preparation into a social event." *In the event that one has control over the family meal*, one can spice things up by incentivizing each member of the family to show off their culinary talents by fixing their own special recipe for the family meal and to do this together in one setting. Doing so transforms the meal preparation event from a "maintenance" type of activity into a "flourishing" activity. The idea is to do this when there is no deficit in meal preparation – you have all the meals ingredients, equipment, space, and family members who can contribute to the meal preparation business.

## Personal Conditions

In personality psychology, there is a theory that has gained much prominence in the psychological literature, it is called *regulatory focus theory* (Higgins, 1997). The theory proposes that we are motivated by two different needs: the need for nurturance versus security. Behavior motivated by nurturance is referred to as "promotion focused." Promotion-focused behavior is concerned with ideals, advances, aspirations, and accomplishments. That is, the behavior is designed to seek positive outcomes. By contrast, behavior motivated by security is referred to as "prevention focused." Prevention-focused behavior is concerned with protection, safety, and responsibility. That is, the behavior is designed to avoid negative outcomes. Innately promotion-focused people tend to be eager in engaging in tasks most likely to produce positive outcomes. By contrast, innately prevention-focused people tend to be vigilant in engaging in tasks well suited for protection, safety, and responsibility.

People who are prevention focused are likely to favor maintenance-type of activities in various life domains, whereas those who are promotion focused are likely to favor flourishing-type of activities. Maintenance activities across all life domains tend to involve vigilance, protection, safety, and responsibility, whereas flourishing activities tend to be driven by ideals, advances, aspirations, and accomplishments. Although there may be personality differences that favor maintenance versus flourishing activities, the advice to the reader is to do both, irrespective of your personality and disposition. Hence, although prevention-focused individuals are likely to gravitate toward maintenance activities, they should incentivize themselves to do what does not come naturally to them, which is to engage in flourishing activities too. Similarly, although promotion-focused individuals are likely to gravitate toward flourishing activities, they should go out of their way to do maintenance tasks to attend to deficits and to ensure stability.

## Societal Conditions

There are many macroconditions that are likely to influence an individual's maintenance versus flourishing actions. Consider the COVID-19 pandemic of 2020–21. This global health crisis has caused a lot of people to become hypervigilant and extremely cautious, while government shutdowns restricted free movement to stop the virus' spread. This prevention-focused behavior dominated every aspect of our lives, not only in health and safety but also in every life domain – family life, social life, leisure life, etc.

The same argument can be made in relation to other "negative" macroconditions such as time of war and conflict; economic downturn and recessions; natural disasters such as hurricanes, tornadoes, and earthquakes; forest fires; and civil unrest. Maintenance activities take precedence over flourishing activities in adverse times such as those. By contrast, flourishing activities can be afforded in times of abundance – when things are going well in the natural, political, economic, and social environment.

## Summary and Conclusion

This chapter focused on how people achieve life balance and maintain an acceptable level of life satisfaction by actively engaging in social roles in multiple domains, specifically domains such as health, love, family, material, social, work, leisure, and cultural life. I described the principle of satisfaction of the full spectrum of human developmental needs – individuals who are satisfied with the full spectrum of developmental needs (i.e., satisfaction of growth needs as well as basic needs) are likely to have a higher level of life satisfaction relative to those who have higher satisfaction but across fewer development needs. When people engage in multiple roles across life domains, they are likely to obtain access to psychological and physical resources, which in turn increase opportunities for the satisfaction of many basic and growth needs. In order to satisfy these developmental needs, individuals engage in a variety of activities to work toward that purpose. The events related to those activities and their outcomes generate a certain amount of satisfaction and dissatisfaction. These affective reactions are organized and stored in memory in certain life domains such as health, love, family, and economics. With respect to growth needs (e.g., social, esteem, self-actualization, self-transcendence, aesthetics, and knowledge needs), experiences may be segmented in life domains such as social life, work life, leisure life, and cultural life. In every life domain, a variety of developmental needs can be met. However, certain life domains are predisposed to meet certain developmental needs more so than others. As such, we argue that health, love, family, and economic domains are likely to reflect satisfaction resulting more from meeting basic than growth needs. Conversely, social life, work life, leisure life, and cultural life are domains likely to reflect satisfaction resulting more from meeting growth than basic needs.

I then described life balance strategies people use in health and safety, love life, family life, material life, social life, work life, leisure life, and cultural life. I made the distinction between maintenance and flourishing strategies that people use in the various life domains. Maintenance strategies are designed to minimize dissatisfaction by meeting basic motivational needs, whereas flourishing strategies are designed to maximize satisfaction by meeting growth needs. Flourishing strategies involve engagement in cultural activities that reflect aspects of one's own personal identity, spirituality, and heritage. To achieve a balanced life, the assertion was made to engage in BOTH maintenance and flourishing activities in health and safety, love life, family life, material life, social life, work life, leisure life, and cultural life.

Following the discussion concerning maintenance versus flourishing activities in the various life domains, I highlighted conditions favorable to maintenance versus flourishing. Specifically, I organized the discussion of these favorable conditions in terms of situational, personal, and societal factors. With respect to situational factors, I argued that situations that highlight deficits in a specific life domain call for maintenance-type of activities. By contrast, nondeficit situations call for flourishing activities. With respect to personal conditions, I used the theory of regulatory focus and hypothesized that prevention-focused individuals (those who are risk averse) are likely to favor maintenance-type of activities in various life domains, whereas those who are promotion focused (those who are not risk averse) are likely to favor flourishing-type of activities. Finally, with respect to societal conditions, I argued that maintenance activities take precedence over flourishing activities in adverse times. By contrast, flourishing activities are afforded in times of abundance – when things are going well in the natural, political, economic, and social environment.

# 5 | *Engagement in New Social Roles*

Several studies conducted by Etkin and Mogilner (2016) provided evidence that *variety* among the activities that fill people's daily lives does, indeed, increase happiness. However, this effect is dependent on the perceived duration of the day. When people have more time (e.g., a full day), varied activities do make a difference in increasing satisfaction. However, when the time is short (e.g., an hour), engaging in varied activities does not contribute to happiness. Actually, in shorter periods, engaging in varied activities may be stressful.

A major national survey (Carlson et al., 2012) found that participation in a *variety* of lifestyle activities helped mitigate impairments in cognitive abilities among older women. Specifically, participation in a greater variety of activities was associated with an 8–11 percent reduction in the risk of cognitive impairment and dementia. Examples of lifestyle activities include things like watching TV, listening to music, listening to radio, going to movies, visiting with friends, gardening, attending religious services, viewing art, cooking, sewing, participating in civic organizations, volunteering, assisting family members, playing games and cards, reading newspapers, discussing politics, singing, drawing, reading books, attending classes, and doing crossword puzzles.

Much research in variety seeking supports the notion that successful engagement in *new* roles is likely to produce more positive affect than successful engagement in well-established roles (e.g., Kahn, 1995; Kahn & Isen, 1993; Levav & Zhu, 2009; McAlister & Pessemier, 1982). That is, engaging in new roles tends to produce a jolt of positive affect much more so than engaging in well-established roles. Also, significant research in industrial/organizational (I/O) psychology has demonstrated the effect of task variety on job performance and employee wellbeing (e.g., Christian, Garza, & Slaughter, 2011; Pierce & Dunham, 1976). That is, compared to workers who are engaged in repetitive tasks, workers engaging in a variety of tasks

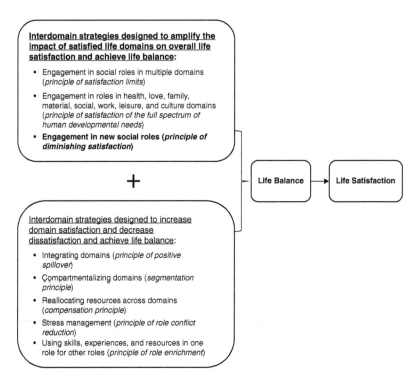

**Figure 5.1** Engagement in new social roles (principle of diminishing satisfaction) to achieve balance

tend to feel much more motivated to excel in their jobs, do much better in terms of job performance, and experience much more job satisfaction. One can extrapolate from this research that life balance is not only limited to engagement in social roles in multiple domains satisfying both basic and growth-related needs but also frequent engagement in new social roles. This may best be explained using the *principle of diminishing satisfaction.* See Figure 5.1.

## The Principle of Diminishing Satisfaction

The principle of diminishing satisfaction states that individuals with life balance are likely to continuously engage in new roles to guard against diminishing satisfaction associated with well-established roles. Why? The intensity of the positive affect experienced in a social role in a given life domain tends to decay because of adaptation effects (Helson, 1964).

Consider the following scenarios: Person A (woman) is right out of college and starting a new job. She experiences success in her professional role. This success is likely to bring much positive affect and satisfaction in work life – +4 units of satisfaction in the work domain – on an 11-point satisfaction scale varying from –5 (very dissatisfied) to +5 (very satisfied). Compare person A to person B (man), who is a seasoned worker – has been on the job for a long time. He is equally successful in his assigned work roles (perhaps +2 units of satisfaction). Yet, man's units of satisfaction are lower because he is not likely to experience the same magnitude of satisfaction compared to the woman. This dampening of positive affect for the man is due to an adaptation effect. That is, positive affect is dampened with repeated successful performance. To guard against this dampening effect and to restore satisfaction in the work life domain to acceptable levels, the man has to engage in new roles to maintain the same level of domain satisfaction that was once generated through now old and well-established role performance.

Research has documented this phenomenon. Previous studies have suggested that people tend to vary the choices they make on a regular basis. For example, when shopping, they seek variety both in the items they choose (e.g., Ratner, Kahn, & Kahneman, 1999; Simonson, 1990) and in the way they choose them (Drolet, 2002). Research has also demonstrated that people perceive a moderate variation in behavior more positively than consistent and habitual behavior (e.g., Simonson, 1989). Moderate variation in behavior is associated with positive and adaptive personal characteristics, such as balance, uniqueness, and varied taste. In contrast, repetitive behavior is associated with negative and maladaptive characteristics, such as rigidity and monotony (e.g., Simonson, 1989).

Consider two individuals, Tom and Anne. Tom just started a new job and has received positive feedback from his supervisor. When asked how he feels about his work life, he replies +5 (on a scale varying from –5 denoting high dissatisfaction to +5 denoting high satisfaction). Anne has an identical job to Tom but has been in that same job for years. She also received the same positive feedback from her supervisor. She reports a +2 on the satisfaction scale. Why? Research has also shown that given successful role performance in a particular life domain (e.g., work life), individuals without a history of satisfaction in that domain are likely to experience a greater magnitude of domain satisfaction than individuals who have a history of satisfaction (e.g., Ahuvia & Friedman, 1998; Diener, Ng, & Tov, 2008; Rojas, 2006). Put succinctly, increases in satisfaction in a life domain serve to increase life satisfaction *but at a decreasing marginal rate with repeated experiences.*

We can capture the preceding discussion in terms of the following prescription: Individuals should become engaged in new social roles in order to mitigate decreases in domain satisfaction and life satisfaction overall. This effect is due to the diminishing satisfaction effect. Specifically, individuals who are engaged in social roles experience diminishing satisfaction in a given life domain over time, which in turn detracts from life satisfaction overall. To guard against this diminishing domain satisfaction, they must engage in new social roles to generate new satisfaction thereby compensating for the diminished satisfaction related to the old roles.

## Strategies of Engagement in New Social Roles and Activities

One can think of new roles and activities by breaking things down by life domain, as we have done in the previous chapter: health, love, family, material, social, work, leisure, and culture. Here are ideas that may inject novelty into your life, thereby decreasing the likelihood of diminishing domain satisfaction (Table 5.1).

Table 5.1 *Strategies of engagement in new social roles and activities*

| Life domain | Engagement in new social roles and activities |
|---|---|
| Health and safety | *Regular physical exercise*: Join a community sports team for a sport that is relatively new to you. |
| | *Eating well-balanced meals*: Plan variety in meal preparation, exploring a new cuisine. |
| Love life | *Dating and outings*: Break the regular routine in taking your significant other out on a date – different restaurants, different social events, different days of the week, etc. |
| | *Loving making*: Try different places, different positions, different music, exploring different fantasies, etc. |
| Family life | *Daily meal preparation*: Break the routine by alternating roles with your significant other and other family members. |
| | *Household chores*: Again, break the routine by alternating roles with your family members. |
| | *Planning family outings*: Take your family to a new pool, park, or even to new vacation destinations. |

**Table 5.1** (*cont.*)

| Life domain | Engagement in new social roles and activities |
|---|---|
| Material (economic) life | *Shopping at stores*: Try different stores than your usual places, or even try different settings such as local farmers' markets or yard sales.<br>*Buying products*: Explore new brands instead of sticking with the same, old brands. |
| Social life | *Socializing at work*: Break the lunch routine at work by inviting a special coworker to lunch at a restaurant.<br>*Socializing with neighbors*: Instead of meeting regularly with one single neighborhood family, you could expand the social circle by including more neighbors. |
| Work life | *Task variety*: Inject variety into job-related tasks. If you are a supervisor or manager, you can do this by assigning workers varied tasks by rotating people through different positions.<br>*Your job*: Think of and suggest new ideas to your supervisor to improve the status quo, volunteer to take on new projects or roles in order to increase task variety. |
| Leisure life | *Weekend leisure*: Plan different weekend outings that are new and exciting.<br>*Vacationing*: Plan vacations to locations that you have never been to, or go with new companions. |
| Cultural life | *Cultural activities*: Introduce variety into cultural activities designed to learn about your own culture and the culture of other people in other places by visiting different museums, watching new historical movies, traveling to different places that have significance to your own heritage, history, and religion (and perhaps the heritage, history, and religion of other people that matter to you). |

## Engaging in Novel Roles and Activities in Relation to Personal Health

What do you do to maintain or enhance a healthy lifestyle? Perhaps you engage in physical exercise and eating a well-balanced diet. Let us say you play racquetball three times a week with the same partner. How can you introduce a little variety in your racquetball routine? Perhaps you can make arrangements with your racquetball partner to join a racquetball club. Doing so allows you to play with different partners on a regular basis. Making this change should prevent the slide of diminishing satisfaction in your exercise routine.

Consider the following study on exercise (Sylvester et al., 2016). The study examined the effects of experiencing variety in exercise among physically inactive college students. A group of inactive students ($N$ = 120) were randomly assigned to follow a high or low variety exercise program for six weeks. Students in the high exercise variety condition participated in the exercise program for a longer duration than those in the low-variety condition. Those in the high-variety condition experienced a sense of variety, which perhaps indicates that the sense of variety in exercising is essential to exercise satisfaction.

How about planning family dinners to ensure there is little or no diminishing satisfaction in this aspect of your personal health. You plan variety in meal preparation. Perhaps you introduce variety into the family dinner by planning different ethnic cuisines for every day of the week: Italian recipe for Monday, Thai food for Tuesday, the Mediterranean for Wednesday, French for Thursday, Friday is leftovers from the previous days, Saturday is eating out at the local steak house, and Sunday is junk food night while watching football.

### Engaging in Novel Roles and Activities in Love Life

What do you do to maintain and enhance your love life? Perhaps you have settled on a routine of going out Saturday evening for a nice dinner after which you return home and make love. Can you do better by introducing novelty into this routine? Perhaps you can plan different types of outings every Saturday. So, every Saturday could be a different outing: a get-together you're your friends for a social event, see a live show in your neighborhood theater, attend a book club gathering at your local library, playing a card game with your favorite friends, visiting with friends at a social club, visiting relatives, going out of town for a romantic getaway, etc. There are endless possibilities.

How about being romantic in bed? How can you break the routine and introduce novelty in this department? One night you may focus on a nice massage in your whirlpool tub. Instead of having sex at night, perhaps you can alternate and make love after you get up in the morning one week at night and another week in the morning. Try different lovemaking positions, different places, different fantasies, and different music?

Consider the following study by Frederick et al. (2017). The study surveyed a very large sample ($N = 38,747$) of adult couples who had been together for at least three years to identify factors related to passion and sexual satisfaction. The study found that a decline in passion and sexual satisfaction is typical. Most respondents reported that they were satisfied with their sex lives during their first six months of relationship. Those who expressed higher levels of sexual satisfaction reported that they had sex more frequently, engaged more in oral sex, had more orgasms, and injected *more variety in sexual acts*, mood setting, and communication about their love life.

You may even explore nontraditional sex. This may involve exploring sexual fantasies that could include anything from role play to BSDM (Bondage, Discipline, Sadism, and Masochism). Other forms of nontraditional sex might involve some form of sexual non-monogamy, such as an open relationship or threesome. Most importantly, engaging in any type of non-monogamous activity is a joint decision with your partner and should only be acted upon after a healthy discussion and agreement. Open relationships and non-monogamous relationships are increasing in popularity in the Western world (Weisman, 2020). Please note that this advice comes with a disclaimer and a caveat. Engaging in nontraditional sexual encounters may wreak havoc in your life because it can create adverse conditions in other life domain that ultimately may take a toll on your subjective wellbeing. To minimize the risk, please educate yourself about the good, the bad, and the ugly about nontraditional sexual behavior. Take advice from mental health professionals who have studied the clinical ramifications of this behavior (Brito & Kassel, 2020; LaBier, 2019).

## Engaging in Novel Roles and Activities in Family Life

A study conducted by Landerholm and Lowenthal (1993) examined the parents' involvement in family activities with their children (e.g., making dinner, helping children with computer-related tasks, and school homework). Of these activities, they compared which activities were most successful. A total of 71 parents participated in the study. Results indicated that the more parents participated in a *variety* of family activities, the more likely they were to feel a strong sense of family wellbeing and overall life satisfaction.

What do you do to maintain and enhance your family life? Let's say you have an established routine for the weekdays and another routine for the weekend. The weekday routine involves the father preparing breakfast for the entire family and dropping off the kids at school. The mother picks up the kids from school and prepares dinner for the whole family. After dinner, both parents spend some time helping the kids with their homework. After homework, each family member does their own thing for entertainment. The kids play games with their friends on the Internet. The parents watch their favorite television shows. The weekends are different. The family usually gets together with other families in the neighborhood or perhaps with other relatives.

Good, yes; but you can do better by breaking up the daily and weekly routine. Perhaps the parents alternate the morning and after-school routine during the week. Instead of the father making breakfast and dropping off the kids at school every morning, you alternate. One week the father does this and another week the mother assumes this role. Conversely, instead of having the mother pick up the kids and prepare dinner during the week, the father may assume this role and alternate week in and week out. With respect to weekends, you can introduce more variety in family life by planning a variety of family events: attending a social event with the entire family, eating out and going to a movie, participating in a sporting event, etc.

We have a friend who periodically rearranges the furniture in the living room to inject novelty and variety into her home life. It seems that every time my wife and I visit with her family we see something different in the living room, rearrangement of the furniture, new artwork, new furniture on the patio, and all types of other renovations. It is her way of spicing up her home life.

## Engaging in Novel Roles and Activities in Material (Economic) Life

Let's talk about shopping. Your weekly shopping routine is to go to the grocery store located in your neighborhood every other day to buy household goods and groceries. Again, perhaps you can break up this routine and, instead of shopping at your local supermarket, you visit another supermarket while driving from place of work to home. Check it out. Perhaps they have food/beverage items that you may find exciting. Or perhaps instead of buying your products at your usual grocery store, instead go to your local farmers market. Consider variety in shopping malls. There is research evidence suggesting that store variety is a significant factor in consumer choice of shopping centers (Oppewal, Timmermans, & Louviere, 1997).

The same goes for shopping for goods at department stores and specialty stores. Instead of shopping at your neighborhood shopping mall, you may try a different one, perhaps in the adjacent district. If you typically rely on online shopping, try visiting physical stores instead.

When buying a product at a store, most consumers are brand loyal. That is, they buy the same brand over and over. Why? Perhaps they do this because of sheer habit, or perhaps they feel that their chosen brand is better or "proven." This is fine of course, but you should try a different brand occasionally. Maybe try the store label instead of the tried company brand. Find out if the store label brand is as good as the national brand, and perhaps you can also save money doing this.

## Engaging in Novel Roles and Activities in Social Life

Professor Bonnie Erickson (2003) makes a case of the benefits of variety in social networks. Variety in social networks means that your circle of people you interact with includes family members, friends, colleagues and coworkers, neighbors, schoolmates, members of social clubs, and other groups you belong to. These social contacts include people of different ages, sex, race and ethnicity, education, nationality, religion, etc. Professor Erickson argues that variety in social life is good because it increases one's chances of getting a good job, helps develop a range of cultural interests, and adds a significant dimension to feeling in control of one's life and health. The key point is that the variety of acquaintances, not necessarily the mere number of social contacts, makes a difference in wellbeing. Moreover, recent research in gerontology – the science that focuses on mature adults and their wellbeing (Fingerman et al., 2020) – has demonstrated that social integration (i.e., involvement with a diverse array of social ties) is associated with a host of positive outcomes including better physical health and wellbeing. More specifically, involvement with diverse social ties is associated with a better mood.

For example, the daily routine in your social life is to have lunch with your work friends. You and your coworkers bring lunch from home and assemble in the lounge room at the office. It's pleasant and familiar. You chat about your family and your leisure activities. Gossip about other people is also interesting. Good, yes, but perhaps occasionally you can do something different for lunch. You can invite a different coworker to a local restaurant to try out an exotic dish. Or perhaps invite a couple of your coworkers for a walk in the park to enjoy the outdoors and eat something at the park.

Or you get together every month with your neighbors. You alternate, one month their place and another your place. This is, of course, great. But how about bringing in another neighbor to your social circle and perhaps doing the same, namely alternating the social gathering. Try finding a new social group to socialize with regularly, such as joining a book club or a trivia team. This can add more spice to your social life.

## Engaging in Novel Roles and Activities in Work Life

Most organizations have a profile sheet for every position in the company. This job sheet defines the various tasks and responsibilities that are tied to each position. In many cases, the tasks are limited to specialized functions. A worker taking on a job must deliver based on those tasks and responsibilities. The job performance of a worker is then evaluated based on the expectations spelled out in the job sheet. In most cases, the job involves a set of repetitive tasks.

There is a well-established model in I/O psychology called "job characteristics" (Hackman & Oldham, 1974, 1976; Hackman et al., 1975). The model focuses on designing a job to enhance motivation and ultimately performance. The model asserts that job motivation and satisfaction are partly determined by five core job features: task significance, *task variety*, task identity, autonomy, and feedback. What concerns us most here is the task variety dimension of the model. A job can be designed to maximize job motivation and satisfaction by increasing the variety of tasks inherent in the job.

Let's consider Jane. She is a wife and mother of a lower-middle-class family. Her husband works in construction, and she works at a supermarket as a cashier. Day in and day out she operates the cash register. When she started this job, she was apprehensive. She was learning how to work the cash register and trying not to make mistakes. Eventually, she mastered the job and felt excited about doing so. This task, as you know, involves quite a bit of repetition – scanning every item for every client all day long. After a year or so, her excitement began to wane. One day she was approached by her supervisor and was told that she will be trained to do other things on the floor (e.g., bagging groceries, stocking items, greeting customers, staffing the customer service desk) and desk-related tasks (e.g., inventory control, procurement, managing and disposal of out-of-date items, work scheduling). Although apprehensive at first, she embraced the new challenge. Eventually, she got very excited about engaging in new tasks and learning the job specification of each position. Doing so added a significant dimension of satisfaction in her work life.

Besides injecting task variety in your job, you can inject novelty in your work life by changing jobs if you are unsatisfied or by improving your current job. You can do the latter by suggesting new ideas to your supervisor to improve the status quo, volunteer to take on new projects or roles within the firm, or perhaps you may apply for a more challenging job within the same company. Doing so may be tumultuous but certainly may add more spice to your work life.

## Engaging in Novel Roles and Activities in Leisure Life

Variety in leisure life also can go a long way to prevent diminishing satisfaction. Consider a study conducted by professors Dimmock et al. (2013). Their study has demonstrated that expectations for task variety influenced interest, enjoyment, and locus of causality in a novel exercise setting. This study compared two groups: One group involved study participants who were exposed to a description of an exercise class that has variety in the type of exercise routine, and the other group was exposed to a description of another exercise program involving similar exercise routine. The first group (those exposed to variety in exercise routine) reported that they would enjoy the class more, could find it more interesting, and more fulfilling, compared to the second group (those exposed to an exercise program involving less variety).

The obvious lesson here is to inject variety into your leisure life. You can easily do this by planning different venues for your vacations and time-off work. Instead of taking the same-old family vacation visiting your in-laws or other relatives, change the venue and do something different. Perhaps plan an ocean cruise for your next vacation. How about a zoo, a circus, an amusement park? How about camping at a state park? Use your imagination. Vacation spots are limitless.

### Engaging in Novel Roles and Activities in Cultural Life

As previously stated, cultural life is about intellectual and emotional experiences related to culture – one's own culture or the culture of others. I mentioned examples including watching a movie that has a major historical element; visiting another country; and experiencing its culture in terms of food and beverage, language, religion, art, and traditional customs and rituals.

Remember Barbara's situation described in Chapter 4. To reiterate, Barbara and her life partner, Sarah, visit the National Museum of the American Indian, a major cultural icon of the history of American Indian in the United States. Barbara is an American Indian descendent, and Sarah is of Anglo descent. Visiting the museum was highly educational for both and a cultural experience. However, the experience has been more rewarding for Barbara than Sarah given her historical roots in the American Indian community. Every year, Barbara and Sarah visit their adopted daughter who lives in Tysons Corner, next to Washington, DC; and every year they visit the National Museum of the American Indian. It has been five years. Should they visit the same museum next year? Perhaps not. This time Barbara would gather her daughter and her family to watch American Indian history movies (e.g., Dances with Wolves, The Last of the Mohicans, Bury My Heart at Wounded Knee, Little Big Man, Pocahontas, and Reel Injun). These movies are not only exciting to watch but also are educational for the entire family, especially the grandchildren. Knowing that her daughter's family is learning about their cultural roots is likely to bring much satisfaction to Barbara's cultural life and, of course, prevent diminishing satisfaction if she were to repeatedly visit the National Museum of American Indian.

### Conditions Favorable to Engagement in New Social Roles and Activities

In this section, I will describe examples of conditions that favor circumstances that call for new roles and activities. These conditions are related to situational, personal, and macrofactors. See Table 5.2 for a summary of these factors.

Table 5.2 *Conditions favorable to engagement in new roles and activities*

| Condition category | Variables |
| --- | --- |
| Situational conditions | Satisfaction deficits in specific life domains and new opportunities to increase domain satisfaction could prompt an individual to engage in new roles and activities. |
| Personal conditions | People high in need for uniqueness are more likely to feel motivated to engage in new roles and activities, compared to those low in that need. |
| Societal conditions | Engaging in novel activities is likely to be more favored in individualistic countries than in collectivistic ones. |

## Situational Conditions

Some situations make people realize that they are experiencing diminishing satisfaction. Eating spaghetti for dinner every few days gets tiring. Your enjoyment of the spaghetti dinner is waning. This is a deficit underlying diminishing satisfaction in your personal health life or perhaps family life (for those who have a nuclear family in the traditional sense). You need to spice things up.

Then, there are many situations that motivate people to try something new. Here is an example, a new restaurant opens in your neighborhood. You feel the urge to try the new restaurant. How about a new neighbor who moved in next door? Wouldn't you feel the urge to meet the newcomers? There is a new update on your cellphone, would you be curious to test it? These are situations that shout at you to try something new.

## Personal Conditions

There may be individual differences that may make novelty seeking more appealing to some more than others. Consider the need for uniqueness (Tian, Bearden, & Hunter, 2001). Individuals who value uniqueness often would like to present themselves as unique and different from others. They differentiate themselves from others by engaging in new behaviors that are markedly different from others. Doing so allows them to show that they are "special." They show distinction by displaying variation in their behavior and engaging in novel activities.

There is a personality measure called the Need for Uniqueness Scale (Tian, Bearden, & Hunter, 2001). Example survey items include: "Often when buying merchandise, an important goal is to find something that communicates my uniqueness"; "The more commonplace a product or brand is among the general population, the less interested I am in buying it." Individuals who score high on this uniqueness scale are likely to engage in new behaviors and roles, and more actively seek out novel activities.

## Societal Conditions

There are macrofactors that may influence people in their choice to engage in variety-seeking behavior. Consider the following study conducted by Kim and Drolet (2003). They conducted three experiments that examined whether the tendency to engage in variety-seeking behavior depends on the cultural context. They were able to demonstrate that people in individualistic cultures (e.g., most of the Anglo cultures such as the United Kingdom, the United States, Australia, New Zealand) tend to value uniqueness and self-expression, much more so than collectivistic cultures (e.g., most Asian cultures such as China, Japan, South Korea). The drive for uniqueness may influence variety-seeking behavior. As such, engaging in novel activities is likely to be more favored in individualistic countries such as the United States (and other countries dominated by an Anglo culture) than in collectivistic cultures. Nevertheless, even when one's culture does not favor novelty and variety seeking, the advice is still to find ways to engage in novel activities as means to offset the diminishing satisfaction of habits.

## Summary and Conclusion

This chapter focused on how people engage in new roles and activities in order to achieve life balance and maintain acceptable levels of life satisfaction. I argued that life balance is not only limited to engagement in established social roles in multiple domains satisfying both basic and growth-related needs but also in experiencing *new* social roles. I explained this tendency through the principle of diminishing satisfaction. This principle states that individuals with life balance are likely to continuously engage in new roles to guard against diminishing satisfaction associated with well-established roles. This occurs because the intensity of the positive affect in the context of a social role experienced in a given life domain tends to decay due to adaptation effects.

I then described strategies that people use to engage in new roles and activities by breaking things down by life domain: health, love, family, material, social, work, leisure, and culture. Specifically, in relation to health and safety, I advised the reader to introduce a little variety in their physical exercise routine (regular physical exercise). I also recommended planning variety in meal preparation (eating well-balanced meals). With respect to love life, the advice is to break the regular routine when going on dates with your significant other – different restaurants, different social events, different days of the week, etc. (dating and outings). In regard to sex, the advice is to try different places, different positions, different music, etc. With respect to family life, I urged the reader to break the regular routine of daily meal preparation and household chores by alternating roles with your family members. Injecting variety in planning family outings is recommended. With respect to material life, I urged the reader to try different stores to inject novelty in shopping and try different brands instead of sticking with the same, old brand. With respect to social life, the advice is to break the lunch routine at work by inviting a special coworker to lunch at a restaurant (socializing at work). Instead of meeting regularly with this one neighbor family, the reader is advised to expand the social circle by including more neighbors. With respect to work life, the advice is to inject variety into job-related tasks. Also, if the reader is a supervisor or holding a management position, I advised that person to assign workers varied tasks by rotating workers through different positions. I also mentioned that if the reader has been working for this one employer in the same old job for a long time, perhaps it's time to inject variety by suggesting to management new projects, new ideas, and new tasks to improve the status quo and thus introduce variety in work life. Or perhaps move to another job within the same organization or even to a new organization. With respect to leisure life, the recommendation is to plan different weekend outings and select different vacation spots. Finally, with respect to cultural life, the reader can introduce variety into cultural activities designed to learn about one's own culture and the culture of other people in other places by visiting different museums watching historical movies, traveling to different places that have significance to one's own heritage, history, and religion (and perhaps the heritage, history, and religion of other people that are important to the reader).

# PART III

# Interdomain Strategies to Increase Domain Satisfaction and Achieve Balance

So far, I have discussed behavioral strategies designed to amplify the impact of satisfied life domains on overall life satisfaction, with the goal of achieving life balance. Now we turn to a different set of behavioral strategies, strategies designed to increase domain satisfaction and decrease dissatisfaction – again, the goal is to achieve balance in life. Specifically, I will discuss five interdomain strategies designed to

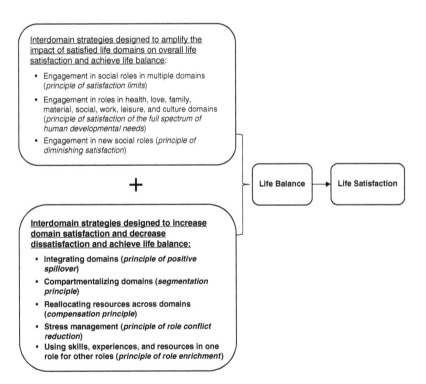

**Figure P3.1** Interdomain strategies designed to increase domain satisfaction and decrease dissatisfaction and achieve balance

increase domain satisfaction and decrease dissatisfaction. These are: (1) integrating domains with high satisfaction (explained by the principle of positive spillover); (2) compartmentalizing domains with low satisfaction (explained by the segmentation principle); (3) reallocating resources across domains (explained by the compensation principle); (4) stress management related to role conflict (explained by the principle of role conflict reduction); and (5) using skills, experiences, and resources in one role for other roles (explained by the principle of role enrichment). See Figure P3.1.

# 6 | *Integrating Domains with High Satisfaction*

Integrating life domains that house high levels of positive affect (or satisfaction) is yet an important personal strategy to help achieve life balance and enhance subjective wellbeing. Doing so serves to maintain life satisfaction at acceptable levels. Consider the owner of a mom and pop store whose family residence is situated on the top floor of the store. His wife and children help at the store by staffing the checkout stand, maintaining inventory, dealing with suppliers and customers, etc. In this situation, the store owner's work life is highly integrated with his family life, marital life, social life, material life, and perhaps community life too. The store is highly successful in that it has a good stream of patrons, a good reputation in the neighborhood, and it generates a decent income that supports his family and a few other jobs in the community. Success in these varied roles translates into positive affect in work life, family life, marital life, social life, material life, and community life. Thus, life satisfaction is increased by integrating both work and family life, which serves to increase satisfaction in both domains. This phenomenon is essentially known as "positive spillover," which will be discussed in some detail in the next section of this chapter. The positive spillover effect does not address a situation involving satisfaction in one domain but dissatisfaction in another (e.g., the store is financially successful but caused problems in marital life because husband and wife have been fighting over how to manage the inventory of the store). This situation may involve a mix of positive and negative spillover, which is not addressed in this chapter. The mix of positive and negative spillover could best be addressed in terms of role conflict, which is the topic of Chapter 10.

Two related and highly similar theories dealing with the management of boundaries between life domains addressed the concepts of domain integration and positive spillover, namely *boundary theory* (Ashforth, Kreiner, & Fugate, 2000; Nippert-Eng, 1996) and *work–family border theory* (Clark, 2000). Boundary theory focuses on work and *nonwork* domains, whereas work–family border theory focuses more particularly on work and *family* domains. These theories make the case that people create psychological boundaries between work and nonwork domains. Some create boundaries to segment domains, while others create more permeable boundaries to allow integration of roles. Our focus here is integration. Specifically, the strength of boundaries refers to the level of flexibility and permeability of the domain boundaries. Flexibility refers to the extent to which a mental boundary contracts or expands in time and space depending on the demands felt in one domain or the other. For example, an individual may erect a work domain boundary with high flexibility (in terms of space and time) to allow him/her to work outside of both his traditional workspace and work time. By contrast, permeability refers to the degree to which affect experienced in domain can spill over to another domain. For example, an individual may segment work and family domains in such a way to prevent bad feelings from family life from spilling over into work life or the other way around. As such, segmentation is viewed as one polar extreme on a continuum with integration on the other extreme. In relation to segmentation (one polar extreme along the segmentation–integration dimension), boundaries between work and family domains are highly impermeable and least flexible. Conversely, the opposite is true in relation to integration (the other polar extreme of the segmentation–integration dimension). That is, in integration, we see the same boundaries as highly permeable and most flexible. Integration allows the individual to easily transition between work and family domains. This is the key benefit of integration.

Let us further delve into this discussion of positive spillover. Experiences in work *and* nonwork life may spill over. That is, affect may spill over from work life to nonwork life, and vice versa. This is what industrial/organizational psychologists commonly refer to as "affect spillover" (e.g., Edwards & Rothbard, 2000; Grzywacz & Carlson, 2007). *Affect spillover* can be either positive or negative. Positive affect spillover refers to positive mood that transfers from one life domain to another. Conversely, negative spillover refers to negative mood spilling over from one domain to another.[1]

---

[1] Affect spillover should be distinguished from *crossover effects*. Affect spillover refers to feelings caused by experiences in one life domain influencing another life domain. It is an intraindividual phenomenon (i.e., within an individual). By contrast, *crossover effect* is an interindividual construct. It refers to an emotional contagion between individuals whereby individuals are influenced

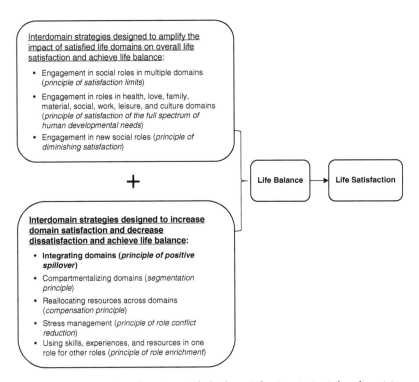

**Figure 6.1** Integrating domains with high satisfaction (principle of positive spillover)

Consider the following case involving two individuals, Mike and Tom. Both men experience "+1" units of satisfaction in work life and "+3" units of satisfaction in family life. However, Tom decides to integrate work and family domains (e.g., by doing work at home and taking care of family responsibilities at work). Tom was highly successful in integrating work and family domains. Doing so increased his satisfaction in work life from "+1" to "+3," whereas his satisfaction in family life remained at "+3." Tom achieved work-life balance through positive spillover. By contrast, Mike did not bother to integrate the two domains; hence, he continued experiencing "+1" satisfaction in work life and

by the emotions displayed by those around them (e.g., Demerouti, Bakker, & Schaufeli, 2005; Hatfield, Cacioppo, & Rapson, 1994). Crossover effects are likely to be high when individuals are in physical proximity and close communications (Barsade, 2002; Neumann & Strack, 2000).

"+3" in family life. In this case, positive spillover through domain integration resulted in greater satisfaction in family life for Tom and as a result higher subjective wellbeing. See Figure 6.1. Please note that I am not implying that integrating work life and family life is *always* a good thing. Toward the end of the chapter, I will discuss conditions when integration is most favorable to achieve balance and enhance wellbeing.

## The Principle of Positive Spillover

The *principle of positive spillover* states that positive affect in two life domains that are highly integrated amplify domain satisfaction, which in turn spills over to overall life satisfaction. That is, positive affect that spills over between life domains increases the level of satisfaction in both of those domains. For example, sharing positive work experiences increases family satisfaction because the act of sharing positive events facilitates positive mood among family members and thus increases family satisfaction (e.g., Gable et al., 2006; Heller & Watson, 2005). Furthermore, positive affect in one role can boost the level of motivation and energy to engage in another role in a neighboring domain. Thus, positive affect in one domain may increase the likelihood of successful performance in a different domain, resulting in increased satisfaction in that domain, which in turn increases life satisfaction overall (Edwards & Rothbard, 2000). In other words, increased satisfaction in the respective domains contributes additively to life satisfaction.

In sum, the preceding discussion can be captured as follows: Individuals who experience positive spillover between two or more life domains through domain integration are likely to experience greater satisfaction in those domains, compared to those who do not experience positive spillover. Such increase in domain satisfaction contributes to life balance by increasing or maintaining life satisfaction at an acceptable level.

## Integration Strategies

There are several integration strategies that have been researched in the literature of industrial/organizational psychology. These include telework, the use of information communication technologies (ICTs), and participating in the gig economy. See Table 6.1.

**Table 6.1** *Domain integration strategies*

| Strategy | Principle |
| --- | --- |
| Teleworking | People who telework have a greater opportunity to exercise psychological integration between and among life domains compared to those who do not telework. |
| Use of information and communication technologies (ICTs) | The use of ICTs can help those who use an integration strategy to maintain life balance. ICTs allow people to move from one role to another, one life domain to another, more frequently and effortlessly. |
| Participating in the gig economy | Work-life balance can be achieved by participating in the gig economy because workers have more freedom to schedule work and nonwork tasks. |

## Teleworking

People who telework have a greater opportunity to exercise psychological integration between and among life domains compared to those who do not telework. Researchers have increasingly studied teleworking in order to understand its impact on work–family conflict (e.g., Bailey & Kurland, 2002; Kurland & Bailey, 1999; Mann & Holdsworth, 2003; Gajendran & Harrison, 2007). Telework may take place during regular office hours as well as outside regular office hours ("after hours") and is considered an alternate work method. Telework should not be confused with "supplemental work" or "overtime."

Telework, as an integration strategy, tends to decrease work-to-family conflict (the type of stress originating from work and spilling over into family life) due to increased flexibility and control over the pacing and scheduling of work as well as increased time at home (e.g., Duxbury, Higgins, & Mills, 1992; Duxbury, Higgins, & Thomas, 1996; Jostell & Hemlin, 2018). However, there may be situations in which integration may be a source of work-to-family conflict – stress from work spilling over to family life. Telework brings down the border between work and family domains, and this could lead to interference with family affairs due to work demand, which may add to, not diminish, work–family conflict (Allen, Golden, & Shockley, 2015).

Lack of a border between work life and home life may also make it difficult to mentally disengage from work (e.g., Boswell & Olson-Buchanan, 2007; Golden, 2012; Hill et al., 2010), thus contributing to work–family conflict. This point was made earlier in Chapter 2 about the imbalanced life. That is, this is a major cause of an imbalanced life. In the section "Conditions Favorable to Integration," I will discuss conditions under which an integration strategy is suitable. We need to take this discussion to heart to ensure that integration does not lead to imbalance. This is important, and I urge the reader to keep this in mind.[2]

## Use of Information and Communication Technologies

The use of ICTs such as the Internet and smartphones has blurred the boundaries between work life and nonwork life (Colbert et al., 2016; Derks, 2016; Derks et al., 2016; Piszczek, 2017). ICTs allow people to move from one role to another, one life domain to another, more frequently and effortlessly – especially when they use an integration strategy of work-life balance. For example, while working, a person can achieve more integration by easily replying to friends' and family instant messages using his/her smartphones. That is, workers can answer personal messages with little-to-no negative impact on their job performance. Integration of professional and personal lives is increasingly commonplace for many organizations and workers. As such, the use of ICTs can assist in integrating work life with nonwork life.

Consider the following study conducted by Wang, Gao, and Lin (2019). This study examined the role of ICTs in family-to-work conflict and work–family balance satisfaction, and the moderating effect of integration in that process. The study findings indicated that high levels of ICT use led to higher levels of family-to-work interference. That is, the use of ICTs can help those who use an integration strategy to maintain work-life balance, but conversely, the use of ICTs

---

[2] It should be noted that we are experiencing increased teleworking due to COVID. The professional landscape is now irrevocably altered by COVID, more employees than ever now telework, many will likely stay telework even after we are allowed to go back to work.

negatively affects those who use a segmentation strategy to keep their work life separate from personal life.

## *Participating in the Gig Economy*

The gig economy refers to freelance and contract work compared to work through permanent positions (Baldoma Jones, 2020). Examples of participating in the gig economy include driving for a rideshare service such as Uber or Lyft, delivering food through an online delivery service such as Grubhub, Doordash, or Uber Eats, or making and selling crafts on a platform such as Etsy. Working in the gig economy provides a measure of flexibility in regard to work that is often absent in permanent positions. Workers in industries that use computer software and the Internet heavily are ideal for the gig economy. For example, journalists use their personal computers to write stories and copy edit. They can do so from home and at times most convenient to them in ways that may not interfere with other responsibilities. As such, the concept of work-life balance is now reconceptualized to take into account the emerging nature of the gig economy (Kelliher, Richardson, & Boiarintseva, 2019). The rise of gig work allows workers to integrate work life with other life domains, boosting productivity while enabling workers to achieve work-life balance (Malone & Issa, 2013).

Consider the following study that focused on Uber drivers in London (Berger et al., 2019). The study found that most of the drivers, although not earning much as they would in a permanent position, report higher levels of life satisfaction than other workers. The researchers attributed the higher life satisfaction among the drivers to their preferences for flexibility and autonomy, which in turn helped them achieve work-life balance. The study highlighted the importance of nonmonetary factors such as work-life balance in contributing to subjective wellbeing in the gig economy.

## Conditions Favorable to Integration

In this section, I will describe examples of conditions that favor circumstances that call for domain integration strategies. These conditions are related to situational, personal, and societal (or macro) factors. See Table 6.2.

Table 6.2 *Conditions favorable to domain integration strategies*

| Condition category | Factors |
| --- | --- |
| Situational conditions | • Managing a family business<br>• When the degree of family responsibility is high and the business is located in (or close to) the home<br>• When telework is voluntary (does not work well if the telework is involuntary as in overtime) |
| Personal conditions | • Integration work-life ideology (integration is suitable for individuals believing that work and nonwork life should be integrated, not segmented)<br>• Positive core self-evaluations (integration is suitable for individuals who see themselves as capable, worthy, and in control of their lives. They have a more positive outlook on things) |
| Societal conditions | • Individualistic versus collectivistic cultures (integration is more suitable in collectivistic countries, whereas segmentation is more suitable in individualistic countries)<br>• Rise of the gig economy (integration is more suitable in countries where a high percentage of workers are participating in the gig economy) |

## Situational Conditions

Research in industrial/organizational psychology has suggested several factors that may hint at situations that may favor integration. These include managing a family business, the degree of family responsibility as connected to location of the business, and voluntary telework.

Let's start with the *family business*. Individuals are likely to experience spillover of positive affect from one life domain to another when the life domains are interdependent and the roles are integrated (e.g., Greenhaus & Powell, 2006; Ilies, Wilson, & Wagner, 2009). Such is the case in managing a family business. The case has been made that many individuals start their own business in order to achieve a greater work-life balance (Brush, 1992; DeMartino & Barbato, 2003; Heilman & Chen, 2003; Kepler & Shane, 2007; Loscocco, 1997;

Powell & Eddleston, 2013). Managing one's own business can often provide autonomy and flexibility, which in turn may play an important role in work-life balance. As such, integration strategies are most suitable for entrepreneurs managing their own small business. That is, on average, the family business context should encourage integration because the context requires it. It is difficult for managers of a family business to segment their lives into work versus family and keep them separate with impermeable boundaries (Piszczek, DeArmond, & Feinauer, 2018).

Consider the following study conducted by Halbesleben, Wheeler, and Rossi (2012). The study found that higher levels of work–family role integration among work-linked couples (i.e., the two spouses working together in the context of a family business) lead to lower levels of work–family conflict. Meaning that couples who run a business together experience lower work–family conflict when they allow more integration between work life and family life. These findings were based on two samples of employees in a variety of occupations.

Research has also suggested that work-life balance in the context of a family business is heavily influenced by two interdependent factors – *level of family responsibility and the location of the business.* Studies have demonstrated that while male entrepreneurs typically experience greater autonomy and flexibility when managing their own business, female entrepreneurs do not always enjoy the same benefits due to their gender (Parasuraman & Simmers, 2001). For men managing their own business – regardless of the location of that business – work-life balance most often increases. However, women who manage their own business *that is located outside of the home* have been shown to actually experience greater work-life conflict in comparison to when that business is located within the home (Cliff, 1998; Loscocco & Leicht, 1993; Parasuraman et al., 1996). These findings are best explained by the fact that women often put much more time and energy into taking care of the home, in essence, they often have a greater degree of family responsibility – ensuring the routine needs of the family are met, which in turn limits the amount of time and energy they can devote to managing their own business, especially if that business is located outside of the home. We can therefore extrapolate that the location of the family business and the degree of family responsibility – regardless of gender – together influence the level of work-life balance that can be achieved by becoming an entrepreneur.

Those individuals with a high level of family responsibility and whose place of business is at home can achieve a greater level of work-life satisfaction due to integration. For these individuals, using an integration strategy allows them to take care of family responsibilities while almost simultaneously managing their business from home (e.g., Eddleston & Mulki, 2017; Shanine, Eddleston, & Combs, 2019; Wight & Raley, 2009). Thus, integration adds more flexibility for them to attend both family and work needs. An individual with a high level of family responsibility will likely experience greater work–family conflict when working at a family business located outside of the home due to the difficulty of transitioning between these roles (i.e., inability to successfully employ integration).

With respect to individuals who have lower levels of family responsibility and manage their own business, evidence (Shanine, Eddleston, & Combs, 2019) suggests that integration works best regardless of other conditions such as whether the business is located in or outside of the home (business located in the home residence versus another location away from the home which entails some commuting time). Integration also works best whether there is family-to-business support (the extent to which management of the business is supported by family members as in answering the phone and taking messages, scheduling clients, doing the bookkeeping, etc.) or not.

Integration does not work to alleviate work–family conflict if the *telework is involuntary*. Consider the following study involving 251 financial sales professionals (Lapierre et al., 2016). This study found that involuntarily working more hours from home outside of their normal workday (i.e., teleworking) increased rather than decreased work-to-family conflict. In other words, involuntary teleworking can backfire and defeat the original goal – to reduce work–family conflict. In sum, integration works best when the decision to engage in telework is autonomous and voluntary. Of course, the COVID-19 pandemic has forced many people to telework. As such, we will need to qualify these study findings in the age of COVID-19 by making a distinction between involuntary telework that is overtime and involuntary telework that is physical but within normal working hours. The pandemic has forced workers to telework because they are physically unable to go to the office. As such, the study findings do not apply to involuntary telework that is physical. In other words, telework is not likely to be an optimal integration strategy for those who engage in telework that is overtime.

## Personal Conditions

Research has pointed to two important personal factors that may be relevant to the use of integration to achieve work-life balance. These are integration work-life ideology and positive core self-evaluations.

What is integration work-life ideology? I addressed this concept in Chapter 2 dealing with life imbalance. To reiterate, Leslie, King, and Clair (2019) proposed that individuals have beliefs about whether segmentation versus integration is most effective in enhancing personal wellbeing and the wellbeing of others. These are beliefs (i.e., ideologies) regarding whether work life and nonwork life are independent versus interdependent. At one extreme, individuals with a segmentation ideology believe that work life and other life domains should be independent, separated, and compartmentalized by impermeable boundaries. As such, they believe that emotional experiences in one domain do not influence thoughts, feelings, and behaviors in other domains. At the other extreme, individuals with an integration ideology believe that work and other life domains should be interdependent. They are separated only by weak and permeable boundaries. As such, they believe that thoughts, feelings, and behaviors in one domain often influence the thoughts, feelings, and behaviors in other domains. This means that an integration strategy is most suitable for people with and integration ideology – definitely not for people with a segmentation ideology.

The concept of *core self-evaluations* is multidimensional in the sense that it involves several personality traits, namely self-esteem, generalized self-efficacy, locus of control, and emotional stability (Judge, Locke, & Durham, 1997; Judge, Van Vianen, & De Pater, 2004). Individuals with positive core self-evaluations tend to view themselves in positive ways in a variety of situations – they see themselves as capable, worthy, and in control of their lives. They have a more positive outlook. Whereas lower core self-evaluation individuals often see themselves as incapable, unworthy, and lacking in control of their lives. The result is they feel stressed in most situations because they have fewer coping mechanisms (Friede & Ryan, 2005; McNall et al., 2011).[3] Thus, individuals with higher core self-evaluation experience

---

[3] Core self-evaluations are customarily assessed with Judge et al. (2003) 12-item Core Self-Evaluations scale. An example item: "I am confident I get the success I deserve in life." Responses to each item are captured on a 7-point scale from 1 = strongly disagree to 7 = strongly agree.

less work–family conflict (Kammeyer-Mueller, Judge, & Scott 2009) making them ideal candidates for integration.

Michel and Clark (2013) conducted a study showing that individuals scoring high on positive core self-evaluations tended to experience more work–family facilitation (or less work–family conflict) and more integration. That is, when faced with stressors, individuals with higher core self-evaluation are more capable of coping with demands stemming from either work or nonwork; and they use their psychological resources to handle difficult situations. As such, they are more likely to actively seek out and implement strategies involving domain integration in order to maximize functioning in multiple domains.

## Societal Conditions

Consider the following study conducted by Urs and Schmidt (2018). Information technology (IT) workers are in high demand in many countries, and as such, many companies make special provisions to recruit IT workers from abroad (e.g., China, Mexico, and India). The study focused on IT workers who were recruited from overseas and physically relocated to live in the United States. All of the study participants immigrated from countries that rigidly maintained separate work and family boundaries, with little to no integration. The study found that while foreign IT workers had initial difficulties adapting to their new environment, over time, they experienced less work–family conflict in the United States compared to the work situation in their home countries. This research suggests that an integration strategy of work-life balance is likely to be more effective in a cultural environment that supports integration of work life and family life.

Different countries have different cultural values. One of these values involves what cultural anthropologists call individualism versus collectivism. People in individualistic countries (e.g., mostly Anglo countries such as the United States and France) place greater emphasis on personal identity and goals, whereas people in collectivistic countries prefer to act as members of groups and for a common good (Hofstede, 1993). In many collectivistic cultures (countries such as India, China, Brazil, and Turkey), work and family domains are more integrated (boundaries between work and nonwork domains are flexible and permeable) compared to individualistic cultures (e.g., the United States). People in individualistic societies tend to segment their work and nonwork domains more strictly, maintaining strong boundaries that are clearly defined. That is, the work culture in the United States tends to support greater segmentation between work and family domains. An individual's commitment to family does not necessarily conflict with commitment to one's career in countries where family norms support a strong work ethic, thus supporting integration between work life and family life. By contrast, individualistic countries' perception of work tends to conflict with demands arising from family and other nonwork domains. Often collectivistic countries place greater importance on the family unit – strongly valuing family relationships, ancestry, and care – and as such tend to have greater organizational support that focuses on improving family life (such as maternity leave, child care, and flexible time off), which can help achieve work–family balance. By contrast, Americans (characterized by cultural sociologists as "individualistic") often have a "leave one's work at the office" motto, viewing long work hours as sacrificing the family role. People in individualistic societies place much emphasis on work, not family. They focus on themselves, their own aspirations and personal strivings, which usually come at the expense of their family life. Study results have supported this hypothesis (Yang, 2005).

The *rise of the gig economy* is yet another favorable condition for the use of an integration strategy to achieve work-life balance and enhance wellbeing (Baldoma Jones, 2020). ICTs were a huge catalyst in the emergence of the gig economy, allowing workers to allocate tasks flexibly, on the basis of demand and availability (Holtgrewe, 2014). The gig economy has allowed workers to escape the tyranny of the clock – no more subjugation to the inflexibility of production lines and offices. Gig economy platforms are providing workers more control over whether they work or not each hour and minute of the day. Specifically, the 2019 Upwork's Freelancing in America (Upwork and Freelances Union, 2019) estimated that 57 million American workers identify themselves as "freelancers." The size of the freelance population was estimated to make up 35 percent of the US workforce in 2019 – an increase of over 4 million since 2014. Several surveys estimated that 5–9 percent of adult internet users in various European countries report working through gig economy platforms weekly (Huws, Spencer, & Joyce, 2016). An index measuring the use of online gig platforms estimates growth of these platforms at an annual rate of 26 percent globally (Kässi & Lehdonvirta, 2018).

## Summary and Conclusion

In this chapter, I have described the domain integration principle which states that balance can also be achieved by integrating life domains that house high levels of positive affect or satisfaction. Doing so serves to maintain, or increase, life satisfaction at acceptable levels by amplifying satisfaction. That is, life satisfaction can be increased to acceptable levels by integrating both work life and family life, which serves to increase satisfaction in both domains (i.e., positive spillover). This means that positive affect in two life domains that are highly integrated amplify domain satisfaction, which in turn spills over to overall life satisfaction.

I discussed several integration strategies, namely telework, the use of ICTs, and participation in the gig economy. With respect to telework, research has demonstrated that people who telework have a greater opportunity to exercise psychological integration between and among life domains compared to those who do not telework. Research has shown that the use of ICTs can help those who use an integration strategy to maintain life balance as ICTs allow people to move from one role to another – one life domain to another – more frequently and effortlessly. Finally, participating in the gig economy helps workers exert more control over their work schedule with greater autonomy. Control and autonomy help with work-life balance, which in turn contributes to overall life satisfaction.

I then focused on examples of conditions that favor circumstances that call for domain integration strategies, categorized in terms of situational, personal, and societal conditions. With respect to situational conditions, the research points to the following. Domain integration works best when an individual is managing a family business. However, the success of domain integration is dependent on the degree of family responsibility and whether or not the business is located in the home. For those with a higher degree of family responsibility, domain integration works best if the business is located in the home, whereas for those with a lower degree of family responsibility, the location of the business does not matter. Also, integration works better when the telework is voluntary – it doesn't work well if the work is involuntary (involuntary as in workers forced to work overtime from their home to catch up on overdue projects and tasks). With respect to personal conditions, research shows that integration works best for people who have a work-life ideology; that is, integration is suitable for individuals who believe that work life and nonwork life should be integrated, not segmented. Furthermore, integration works best for individuals with positive core self-evaluations; that is, integration is suitable for individuals who see themselves as capable, worthy, and in control of their lives. They have a more positive outlook on things. Integration also works better for individuals living in collectivistic countries, not individualistic countries due to differing societal expectations and pressures. Finally, integration works better in countries with significant participation in the gig economy. The gig economy allows workers to exert greater control over the time they spend working, thus allowing them to spend more time in other life domains.

# 7 | Compartmentalizing Domains with High Dissatisfaction

Consider the following scenario comparing two individuals (persons A and B) who are experiencing dissatisfaction at work: –3 units of dissatisfaction on an 11-point scale varying from –5 (very dissatisfied) to +5 (very satisfied). However, both individuals are satisfied with their family life (+3 units of satisfaction). Both individuals are experiencing negative spillover of affect from work life to family life. That is, their dissatisfaction at work (–3 units of satisfaction) is influencing their mood at home, causing friction and stress in their family life. Person A decides to deal with the high dissatisfaction at work by compartmentalizing their work life to prevent future negative spillover of negative affect from work life to family life. That is, they decide that at home, they will not think about work issues, speak of work issues, and do any work-related activities. By doing so, person A manages to maintain their satisfaction in family life to the previous level (+3). Person B does not segment and thus experiences decreased satisfaction in family life as a result of the negative spillover from work.

Negative affect in one life domain is likely to spill over to other life domains when there is a high level of overlap across life domains in terms of time, space, effort, and resources. In order to prevent spillover of negative affect to other life domains, individuals create and maintain psychological, physical, or behavioral boundaries around their life domains (Ashforth, Kreiner, & Fugate, 2000; Edwards & Rothbard, 2000; Judge et al., 2001; Sonnentag, 2012). For example, workers can segment family life domain from work life domain. At home, they do not converse about work experiences. Work-life issues stay at work, and home-life issues stay at home.

Research by Lucas, Diener, and Suh (1996) has demonstrated that the overall happiness is composed of separable wellbeing variables (e.g., work satisfaction, home satisfaction, and life satisfaction). These variables sometimes move in different directions over time (cf. Scollon & Diener, 2006). This finding points to the possibility that

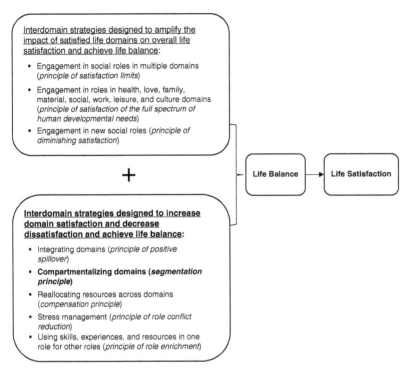

**Figure 7.1** Compartmentalizing domains with low satisfaction (segmentation principle)

some people – at times – are able to prevent spillover of negative affect between life domains. See Figure 7.1.

## The Segmentation Principle

Let us now delve further into the psychological dynamics concerning the effect of segmentation on life satisfaction. Dubin (1958) and Wilensky (1960) were the first to describe how people use segmentation to enhance their subjective wellbeing. They argued that when people feel dissatisfied in one life domain and they realize they have little control in changing that outcome, they try to "seal off" the domain housing the dissatisfaction. They do so to maintain a certain level of overall life satisfaction (i.e., to ensure that overall life satisfaction does not drop below an intolerable level). In essence, affect (i.e., emotions or feelings) from one domain "spills over" into other domains, and people "segment" their affect in certain domains in order to prevent affect from spilling over.

As discussed in Chapter 6, there are two overlapping theories dealing with the management of boundaries between life domains, namely boundary theory (Ashforth, Kreiner, & Fugate, 2000; Nippert-Eng, 1996) and work–family border theory (Clark, 2000). Boundary theory focuses on work and *life* domains, whereas work–family border theory focuses more on work and *family* domains. These theories make the case that people create psychological boundaries between work and nonwork domains. As such, psychological boundaries or borders can vary on a continuum from high segmentation to low segmentation. Specifically, the strength of boundaries refers to the level of permeability of the domain boundaries. Permeability refers to the degree to which emotions experienced in one domain can spill over into another domain. That is, an individual may erect an impermeable boundary between work and family domains in such a way to prevent bad feelings from family life from spilling over into work life or the other way around. By contrast, another individual may have a permeable boundary that allows both positive and negative feelings from work life to flow into family life, and vice versa. As such, high segmentation is viewed as one polar extreme on a continuum with low segmentation the other extreme. For example, a highly segmented person may never bring work home, has no home office, and does not take work calls when at home. This person has a highly impermeable boundary between work life and family life. Whereas a low-segmented person works primarily from home and therefore has a highly permeable boundary between work life and home life.

We know from past studies in industrial/organizational psychology that high permeability between work and nonwork domains is linked to higher levels of work-to-family conflict (e.g., Bulger, Matthews, & Hoffman, 2007; Kossek et al., 2012; Olson & Boswell, 2006) and family-to-work conflict (e.g., Bulger, Matthews, & Hoffman, 2007; Kossek, Lautsch, & Eaton, 2006; Kossek et al., 2012; Kim & Hollensbe, 2017). Work-to-family conflict is the stress an individual may feel at home because of work-related problems. And conversely, family-to-work conflict is the stress experienced at work because of family-related problems.

As such, the *segmentation principle* posits that individuals who segment life domains can prevent spillover of negative affect across life domains – preventing both work-to-family conflict and family-to-work conflict. Segmentation of dissatisfying life domains from other life domains contributes to overall life satisfaction because this practice protects satisfaction in other life domains. Segmentation of a life domain with negative experiences is also important because it serves as a coping mechanism and a buffer for subjective wellbeing. Much research in work-life balance has provided substantial evidence of the segmentation effect (e.g., Edwards & Rothbard, 2000; Medrano & Trogolo, 2018; Michel & Hargis, 2008; Sonnentag et al., 2008; Xin et al., 2018; Zhao et al., 2017). Consider the following meta-analytic study (i.e., a study that analyzes the size across multiple studies) of the effect of work–family conflict by Michel and Hargis (2008). Based on 209 samples and 994 effect sizes, the study indicated that work–family conflict explains 2.20 and 6.20 percent of the variance in job and family satisfaction outcomes, whereas segmentation explains 54.10 and 48.50 percent of the same outcomes, respectively. In layman's terms, this means that work–family conflict is likely to be a strong factor in influencing satisfaction in work life and family life.

The concept of segmentation can be summarized as a behavioral life-balance strategy. Compared to individuals who do not compartmentalize their dissatisfied domains from spilling over to other domains, those who manage to compartmentalize reduce the likelihood of decreases in life satisfaction overall. That is, compartmentalizing negative affect in one domain serves to protect neighboring domains from negative spillover, thus preventing the neighboring domains from slipping into dissatisfaction and doing so prevents overall declines in life satisfaction.

## Segmentation Strategies

Segmentation strategies can be classified into four categories: (1) *temporal* – control time, (2) *physical* – physical boundaries, (3) *behavior* – negotiate boundaries, and (4) *communicative* – managing expectations (Kreiner, Hollensbe, & Sheep, 2009). See Table 7.1 for a summary of these strategies and Table 7.2 for example survey measures (Carlson, Ferguson, & Kacmar, 2016).

### Temporal Segmentation

Temporal segmentation refers to segmentation involving time control (Kreiner, Hollensbe, & Sheep, 2009). In other words, one can

Table 7.1 *Domain segmentation strategies*

| Strategy | Principle |
| --- | --- |
| Temporal segmentation | Segmentation by creating time boundaries: One can segment work life from interference from family life (or vice versa) by making decisions and changes in one's daily calendar. |
| Physical segmentation | Segmentation by physical boundaries: One can insulate a domain by decisions to engage in domain-related activities within specified boundaries that are spatial in nature (e.g., the physical space of home residence becomes the boundary protecting family life). |
| Behavior segmentation | Segmentation by behavior-based boundaries: An example may be the use of two email accounts to separate professional from personal life. |
| Communicative segmentation | Segmentation by managing boundaries with others: An example is to request supervisors and coworkers not to call at home to discuss job-related concerns during nonbusiness hours. |

segment work life from interference from family life (or vice versa) by making decisions and changes in one's daily calendar. For example, one can create an impermeable boundary around family life by deciding that after-work hours are exclusively reserved for family time. No time will be allotted to work-related tasks. Temporal segmentation allows the individual to extract satisfaction from the compartmentalized domain by allocating much more time and energy to activities to that domain and that domain alone. Doing so increases the individual involvement and engagement in that domain, which in turn may result in higher levels of satisfaction in that domain (Beutell & Wittig-Berman, 1999; Myrie & Daly, 2009; Wegge et al., 2007).

Survey items capturing temporal segmentation are shown in Table 7.2. Examples include "While at work, I try to manage blocks of time so that I can keep work separate from family." This item captures temporal segmentation in the work domain to ensure that family

**Table 7.2** *Survey measures segmentation strategies*

- ❖ Keeping family out of work
  - ➢ Work–family: Temporal
    - ▪ While at work, I try to manage blocks of time so that I can keep work separate from family.
    - ▪ While at work, I try to manage my time such that work time is work time, not family time.
    - ▪ While at work, I manage my time to keep family demands out of work.
  - ➢ Work–family: Physical
    - ▪ When I'm physically at work, I try not to address family-related issues so I can focus on work.
    - ▪ When I'm in the workplace, I leave family matters at home so that I can focus on work.
    - ▪ When I walk in the door to work, I put away any family-related thoughts and turn my focus to work.
  - ➢ Work–family: Behavioral
    - ▪ While at work, I use technology to help facilitate keeping work responsibilities separate from family responsibilities.
    - ▪ While at work, I use technology to help keep family demands out of my work life.
    - ▪ While at work, I use technology to help limit dealing with family during work time.
  - ➢ Work–family: Communicative
    - ▪ I communicate clearly to my family that I prefer not to be distracted by family demands while I'm at work.
    - ▪ I have indicated to my family that I cannot deal with family matters during work hours unless it is a rare circumstance.
    - ▪ I set expectations with my family to not contact me at work unless it's an emergency.
- ❖ Keeping work out of family
  - ➢ Family–work: Temporal
    - ▪ While at home, I try to manage blocks of time so that I can keep family separate from work.
    - ▪ While at home, I try to manage my time such that family time is family time, not work time.
    - ▪ While at home, I manage my time to keep work demands out of family.

(*cont.*)

**Table 7.2** (*cont.*)

> ➤ Family–work: Physical
>   - When I'm physically at home, I try not to address work-related issues so I can focus on my family.
>   - When I'm at home, I leave work matters at work so that I can focus on my family.
>   - When I walk in the door at home, I put away any work-related thoughts and turn my focus to family.
> ➤ Family–work: Behavioral
>   - While at home, I use technology to help facilitate keeping family responsibilities separate from work responsibilities.
>   - While at home, I use technology to help keep work demands out of my family life.
>   - While at home, I use technology to help limit dealing with work during family time.
> ➤ Family–work: Communicative
>   - I communicate clearly to my coworkers/supervisors that I prefer not to be distracted by work demands while I'm at home.
>   - I have indicated to my boss that I cannot work past the end of my normal workday unless it is a rare circumstance.
>   - I set expectations with my coworkers/supervisor to not contact me at home unless it's an emergency.

*Source:* Carlson, Ferguson, and Kacmar (2016).

demands would not interfere with work, thereby protecting the work domain from other domains such as family life. "While at home, I try to manage my time such that family time is family time, not work time" is another survey item capturing temporal segmentation of the family domain.

## Physical Segmentation

Recent research has found that the increased use of mobile technologies blurs the boundaries between work and family, making segmentation difficult (Chesley, 2005; Park, Fritz, & Jex, 2011; Schieman & Young, 2013). Today more than ever, we have easy access to work-related platforms, such as email, from our home and mobile devices. This access is designed to enhance our ability to work remotely. This is, of course, both good and bad. The bad thing about this enhanced work accessibility, or what some scholars call "24/7 availability," is the fact that it may generate additional stress in other life domains. Work access at home can add stress by allowing work to intrude upon family life. This is a good illustration of the challenges of physical segmentation in the modern workplace.

To further illustrate, consider the following survey item capturing the physical segmentation of family life: "When I'm physically at home, I try not to address work-related issues so I can focus on my family" (see Table 7.2). This item illustrates how people segment their family life from interference from work by making and implementing the decision to protect the family domain through a physical barrier, the actual home residence. That is, physical segmentation involves attempts to identify spatial boundaries and insulate the domain by decisions to engage in domain-related activities within specified boundaries that are spatial in nature – The physical space of the home residence becomes the boundary protecting family life (Kreiner, Hollensbe, & Sheep, 2009). Thus, the use of physical boundaries in segmenting a given domain allows the individual to focus and experience more satisfaction in that domain as well as be more psychologically engaged in that domain (Carlson, Ferguson, & Kacmar, 2016). As such, to implement physical segmentation, the advice is when you are physically at home, try not to address work-related issues so you can focus on your family. This means strict adherence to physical separation in the home itself – you should only engage in the work while in the home office or other designated workspace. You become engaged in nonwork activities only when you are outside of that space.

*Behavior Segmentation*

Consider the following survey item to capture behavior segmentation in the work domain: "While at work, I use technology to help keep family demands out of my work life" (see Table 7.2). This item shows a specific behavior (e.g., the use of technology to allow the person to focus on work responsibilities and minimize possible interference from family demands [Kreiner, Hollensbe, & Sheep, 2009; Carlson, Ferguson, & Kacmar, 2016]).

For example, using screening calls (i.e., caller ID on your phone) or having two separate calendars or email accounts on one device allows individuals to manage their boundaries. Caller ID allows the individual to identify the caller; if the caller is from work, the individual may reject the call, thereby allowing them to be fully engaged in family life with little interference from work life. How about not answering your work email at home? Here, the segmentation is not only based on the physical space of being at home but also taking concrete action of not responding to work-related communications, *period*. The result of behavioral segmentation is to ensure maximum satisfaction in the family domain (Golden & Geisler, 2007; Park, Fritz, & Jex, 2011). Given the prevalence of technology, behavior-based segmentation is extremely important in regulating work and family domain separation. The use of behavior segmentation that keeps family out of work should contribute to greater job satisfaction and job engagement; and similarly, keeping work out of family should contribute to greater family satisfaction and family engagement.

## Communicative Segmentation

Industrial/organizational psychologists studying work-life balance assert that work contact (i.e., communication with work colleagues related to work matters) represents a "boundary-spanning demand" that blurs the boundaries separating work life from non-work life (e.g., Clark, 2000; Voydanoff, 2005a). This boundary-spanning demand is distinct from job-related demands such as long work hours and excessive pressures (Glavin & Schieman, 2012; Schieman & Glavin, 2008). Work contact, as a boundary-spanning demand, hacks away at the border separating work life from other life domains. As such, it is considered a potential stressor. To alleviate this potential stress, the individual should request that their supervisor and other coworkers refrain from getting in touch with them outside of the workplace or work hours (through any means of direct communication such as phone calls, text messaging, or email) to discuss work-related issues. In most cases, such requests are honored, and it makes it more enforceable when the individual makes such requests explicit, perhaps in writing. This is the essence of communicative segmentation. Of course, in an age of pandemics in which many people work from home, work contact is the new normal. As such, a communicative rule such as "don't communicate with me while I am at home" is not realistic. The best one can do is segment by saying to work colleagues "you can communicate with me by e-mail or text anytime, but I'll respond during work hours and only during those hours."

To reiterate, communicative segmentation involves the management of others' expectations regarding boundaries (Kreiner, Hollensbe, & Sheep, 2009). That is, a boundary is erected by signaling to others that certain actions constitute boundary violations, hence the plea to respect one's boundaries. Consider the following survey item: "I have indicated to my boss that I cannot work past the end of my normal workday unless it is a rare circumstance" (see Table 7.2). Here, the individual has managed to erect a boundary around his/her family domain by communicating to their boss that the home is their sanctuary and to refrain from expecting them to engage in work-related matters during "family time" (possibly evenings and weekends). By communicating their expectations to others (family members, coworkers, and boss), the individual can segment the work and family domains assuming that these expectations are adhered to and violations would not occur. As such, communicative segmentation is likely to contribute to greater engagement in the protected domain, thus ensuring greater satisfaction in the same domain (Carlson, Ferguson, & Kacmar, 2016).

## Conditions Favorable to Segmentation

To maintain consistency with the other chapters, this section focuses on conditions favorable to the use of segmentation in terms of three sets of variables, namely situational, personal, and societal conditions. In other words, we do not recommend the application of segmentation across the board (i.e., in any situation, for all types of individuals, and across all cultures and societies). Conversely, what should be stated here is that segmentation is likely to be optimal under a set of unique situations, for certain type of people, in certain macroeconomic and public health conditions. See Table 7.3.

### Situational Conditions

Research in work-life balance has suggested several factors that may help us identify situations that would encourage segmentation. These

Table 7.3 *Conditions favorable to domain segmentation strategies*

| Condition category | Variables |
| --- | --- |
| Situational conditions | • Role confusion: Segmentation is useful in situations when the individual is motivated to engage in two conflicting roles.<br>• Role attachment: Segmentation is useful when the individual is committed to two conflicting roles.<br>• Cross-boundary interruptions: Segmentation is useful when the individual situated in one domain experiences interference from role demand in another domain.<br>• Family business, gender, and location of business: Segmentation is useful for women managing a family business at a location outside the home.<br>• Organizational segmentation support: Segmentation is useful when the employer supports the notion that work life should be separated from home life.<br>• Workplace ostracism: Segmentation is useful when the individual is ostracized at work. |
| Personal conditions | • High contrast, low permeability, and low flexibility: Segmentation is useful for individuals with boundaries that are high in contrast, low in permeability, and low in flexibility.<br>• Fixed pie (versus expandable pie) work-life ideology: Segmentation is useful for individuals who have a fixed pie work-life ideology, compared to those with an expandable pie ideology.<br>• Segmentation (versus integration) work-life ideology: Segmentation is useful for individuals who have a segmentation work-life ideology, compared to those with an integration ideology. |
| Societal conditions | • Economic recession: Segmentation is useful to shield from the negative spillover stemming from material life unto other life domains.<br>• Pandemics: Segmentation is useful to shield from the negative spillover stemming from health and safety unto other life domains. |

include role confusion; role attachment; cross-boundary interruptions; family business, gender, and location of business; organizational segmentation support; and workplace ostracism.

Segmentation can work best in situations involving issues dealing with role confusion (Ashforth, Kreiner, & Fugate, 2000; Clark, 2000; Nippert-Eng, 1996). Individuals may experience role confusion when they have trouble deciding whether a work or family role should be prioritized in a situation. Let's focus on *role confusion* first. For example, a husband/father takes his family on a beach vacation. The husband/father runs a business and he is on call 24/7. He receives repeated and frequent calls from a business associate regarding work during the vacation and feels compelled to spend significant time and energy over the phone in order to attend to work demands. However, he has already committed to his wife and children to spend the entire day visiting a family attraction. He knows that he would not be able to attend to work demands at the attraction site. What should he do in this situation? Should he assume the role of father and husband and put work demands on hold? Or should he attend to work demands and ask his wife and children to spend the day on their own without him at the attraction site? Segmentation can help in this situation. He could delegate his business associates to deal with all work-related problems while he is on vacation with his family. In other words, he makes an explicit decision that the vacation is family time, and no work demand shall infringe on family time. This is a good segmentation strategy well suited to the occasion.

Research has also shown that segmentation can work best in situations involving issues dealing with *role attachment* (Ashforth, Kreiner, & Fugate, 2000; Clark, 2000; Nippert-Eng, 1996). Role attachment problems are problems related to switching between work and family roles. Consider the same situation – the husband/father on a family vacation. He is attached to both family and work roles. He is totally committed to both roles and invests much time and energy into being a good husband/father as well as a good boss. His most important goal at this stage in life is to make sure his business is successful, and his wife and children are happy and well taken care of. Because he is strongly attached to these two roles, segmentation can help here. Segmentation can play out in this situation by making a decision that vacation time is family time. Work will not interfere with family time.

He delegated work matters to his business associate who will oversee business matters while he is on vacation with his family. This segmentation strategy allows him to devote sufficient time and energy to these two roles in order to ensure successful role performance as both a husband/father and boss. Of course, the catch is to choose a business associate he can trust to make good decisions while he is away on a family vacation.

Segmentation can help with *cross-boundary interruptions* (Ashforth, Kreiner, & Fugate, 2000; Clark, 2000; Nippert-Eng, 1996). Cross-boundary interruptions can be exemplified by the same situation involving the boss taking a family vacation when he knows too well that his vacation and family fun is very likely to be frequently interrupted because of work demands. Anticipating frequent work-related interruptions while is vacationing calls for segmentation. In this situation, he may reassign a role in his department to specifically handle his job while away. He would set an automated away message on his email that routes the questions to the correct contact person.

How about the interaction between *family business, gender, and location of business*? What conditions are most favorable to apply a segmentation strategy to achieve a balanced life? In Chapter 6 (Integrating Domains with High Satisfaction), I described research related to gender and entrepreneurship. I referred to evidence suggesting that life balance can be achieved through integration, especially for women who manage their own business from home (Shanine, Eddleston, & Combs, 2019). Specifically, women expend more time and energy taking care of the home than other family members, which in turn limits the amount of time and energy they can devote to managing their own business. As such, integration works best for women when their place of business is at home. When working from home, they can more easily coordinate work and family responsibilities. However, the same study (Shanine, Eddleston, & Combs, 2019) also suggested that women can achieve life balance through segmentation *when the business is located outside the home* (i.e., an independent business location). When the business is located outside the home, women do better by separating work life from family life. Integrating work life and family life is more effortful, both physically (as in commuting back and forth between home and work) and emotionally (handling the stresses and strains of work and family in different locations). In sum, integration may be key when women have their own business that operates from inside the home. But segmentation is key when a woman has her own business that operates outside the home. One can further appreciate this principle by acknowledging that social norms dictate that it is more imperative for women to attend to family first and perhaps work second. In other words, society mandates that family comes first for most women. Integration does not work well for most women managing a business outside the home because often family demands will trump work demands. And by doing so, women who are trying to integrate work life and family life are likely to do poorly with respect to managing their business because they will turn their attention to family matters at the expense of work matters. Thus, segmentation works best for women who manage their own business outside the home.

*Organizational segmentation support* refers *to* employee perceptions that the organization supports segmentation. That is, the organization encourages its employees to keep work matters at work and not to bring family matters to work. Research has shown that organizational segmentation support contributes to a variety of positive outcomes such as family functioning, organizational commitment, spousal commitment to the organization, and marital satisfaction (Ferguson, Carlson, & Kacmar, 2015).

Consider the study conducted by Liu et al. (2013) in China in relation to *workplace ostracism*. This study involving a three-wave survey of 233 employees treated workplace ostracism as a source of major stress and examined its spillover effects on family life. The researchers found that those individuals who were able to segment work life from family life experienced lower levels of work-to-family conflict, compared to those who failed to segment. That is, those who managed to segment dissatisfaction experienced in work life suffered less work–family conflict; hence, they were able to ensure little or no negative spillover from work life to family life.

## Personal Conditions

Research has suggested that there are at least three personal factors that may highlight conditions favorable to segmentation. These are high contrast, low permeability, and low flexibility; fixed pie (versus expandable pie) work-life ideology; and segmentation (versus integration) work-life ideology.

As previously discussed, Ashforth, Kreiner, and Fugate (2000) theorized that boundaries can vary in three ways: *flexibility, permeability, and contrast*. Flexibility refers to the extent to which a role can be enacted in different settings and times. Permeability refers to the extent to which the individual can be physically located in a role domain but psychologically involved in another role. Contrast refers to the extent to which defining features of an individual's roles are similar or different. For example, a man who manages a business outside the home has to play the role of the manager during the day at his place of work but cannot assume the same role at home in evening hours (low flexibility); the same person performs employee evaluations at work but cannot perform the same function at home (low permeability); and the same person who is both a father (nurturing and kind) and a business person (assertive and demanding) might have very different defining features of the two roles (high contrast). As such, boundary theorists would argue that individuals whose roles are low on flexibility, low on permeability, and high in contrast are most likely to benefit from segmentation. Segmentation is beneficial in that it offers the individual role clarity, a low probability of cross-role distraction, and relative ease of role engagement.

Leslie, King, and Clair (2019) proposed that individuals vary in their belief that resources (time, energy, money, psychological, etc.) for work and nonwork compete – *fixed versus expandable pie work-life ideology*. At one extreme, individuals believe that one has only a finite set of resources that can be used to meet demands in various life domains. For example, one has only so much time in each day. Spending time with family must come at the expense of spending time at work, and vice versa. That is, investment of time to meet work demands depletes time available for other life domains (family, social, leisure, sports and recreation, financial, spiritual, life, etc.). At the other extreme, individuals with an expandable pie ideology believe that some resources (time, money, energy, psychological, etc.) are expandable. For example, one may believe that expressing sympathy and compassion to others is an expandable pie. You can dole it out freely, and the more you dole it out, the more you have more to dole out. The same thing may apply to other resources such as money. The more you dole out money, the more you gain to dole out some more – perhaps being generous with one's money helps one become more successful, which, in turn, helps the person make more money to allow them to become increasingly charitable. The principle here is that segmentation is much better suited for individuals who are high in fixed pie work-life ideology. If you are the type of individual who truly believes that a certain resource (time, money, energy, psychological, etc.) is "fixed" (i.e., once the resource is allocated to some role, the same resource cannot be used to support other roles), then segmentation is best for you to help you achieve life balance.

Leslie, King, and Clair (2019) also proposed that individuals have divided beliefs about whether segmentation versus integration is most effective in enhancing their wellbeing and the wellbeing of others. These are beliefs (i.e., ideologies) regarding whether work and nonwork life are independent versus interdependent. At one extreme, individuals with a *segmentation ideology* believe that work life and other life domains are independent, separated, and compartmentalized by impermeable boundaries. As such, emotional experiences in one domain do not influence thoughts, feelings, and behaviors in other domains. At the other extreme, individuals with an integration ideology believe that work and other life domains are interdependent. They are separated only by weak and permeable boundaries. As such, thoughts, feelings, and behaviors in one domain often influence thoughts, feelings, and behaviors in other domains. Of course, the segmentation implication here is quite clear: Segmentation works best for individuals with a segmentation ideology. Conversely, segmentation does not work well for those with an integration ideology.

## Societal Conditions

There are many macrofactors that induce people to segment their domains with negative feelings (to prevent them from spilling other and infecting neighboring domains). Most are related to resource scarcity. For example, during a downturn of the economic cycle – as in a recession – many organizations cut back by reducing their labor force, consolidating, and increasing work demand on those who are not laid off. These are adverse events that put significant stress on workers. If not contained, the negative feelings that accumulate in work life can easily spill over to other life domains such as family life, social life, financial life, and leisure life. Thus, to maintain work-life balance, people turn to segmentation. Segmenting the negative feelings in work life helps minimize negative spillover to other life domains.

By doing so, the individual manages to maintain an acceptable level of life satisfaction.

A similar argument can be made to other societal conditions such as pandemics. Many have experienced a great deal of adversity because of the surge of COVID-19. Public health has been severely compromised. COVID-19 has created havoc in people's lives. Segmenting the negative feelings resulting from this public health crisis can help maintain an acceptable level of life satisfaction. In other words, one can insulate their feelings related to the pandemic to prevent emotional contagion – mitigate the spillover of negative feelings related to health, the health of loved ones, and the health of the community at large from "infecting" all aspects of our lives. Segmentation can work to achieve life balance under adverse societal conditions.

## Summary and Conclusion

This chapter focused on segmentation – how people create psychological "walls" around life domains that contain negative affect to prevent the spillover of these bad feelings into other life domains. Compared to individuals who do not compartmentalize their dissatisfied domains from spilling over to other domains, those who manage to compartmentalize reduce the likelihood of decreases in life satisfaction overall. That is, compartmentalizing negative affect in one domain serves to protect neighboring domains from negative spillover, thus preventing the neighboring domains from slipping into dissatisfaction and doing so prevents declines in life satisfaction.

The research provides much information about several segmentation strategies that people commonly use, namely temporal, physical, behavior, and communicative. Temporal segmentation involves creating time boundaries. That is, one can segment work life from interference from family life (or vice versa) by making decisions and changes in one's daily calendar. Physical segmentation involves creating physical boundaries. That is, one can insulate a domain by decisions to engage in domain-related activities within specified boundaries that are spatial in nature (e.g., the physical space of home residence becomes the boundary protecting family life). Behavior segmentation involves creating boundaries through specific action. An example may be the use of two email accounts to separate professional life from personal life. Finally, communicative segment refers to negotiating the expectations of others. An example is to request supervisors and coworkers not to call at home to discuss job-related concerns.

I then discussed conditions that are favorable to the use of segmentation strategies. This discussion was broken down into situational, personal, and societal conditions. The established research provides information about a host of factors: role confusion (segmentation is useful in a situation where the individual is motivated to engage in two conflicting roles); role attachment (segmentation is useful when the individual is committed to two conflicting roles); cross-boundary interruptions (segmentation is useful when the individual situated in one domain experiences interference from role demand in another domain); family business, gender, and location of business (segmentation is useful for women managing a family business at a location outside the home); organizational segmentation support (segmentation is useful when the employer supports the notion that work life should be separated from home life); and workplace ostracism (segmentation is useful when the individual is ostracized at work).

With respect to personal factors, the research identified at least three factors under which segmentation is beneficial. These are: high contrast, low permeability, and low flexibility (segmentation is useful for individuals with boundaries that are high in contrast, low in permeability, and low in flexibility), fixed pie (versus expandable pie) work-life ideology (segmentation is useful for individuals who have a fixed pie work-life ideology, compared to those with an expandable pie ideology); and segmentation (versus integration) work-life ideology (segmentation is useful for individuals who have a segmentation work-life ideology, compared to those with an integration ideology).

With respect to societal factors, the discussion focused on the effects of economic recession and pandemics: economic recession (segmentation is useful to shield from the negative spillover stemming from material life unto other life domains) and disease pandemic (segmentation is useful to shield from the negative spillover stemming from health and safety unto other life domains).

# 8 | *Reallocating Resources across Domains*

Research suggests that individuals feeling dissatisfied with their jobs allocate more resources to more satisfying nonwork activities such as leisure, family, or religion (e.g., Brief et al., 1993; Freund & Baltes, 2002; Judge et al., 2001; Tait et al., 1989). Consider the following study by Best, Cummins, and Lo (2000) specifically. These researchers conducted a study on the quality of rural and metropolitan life and found that both groups report equivalent levels of life satisfaction. However, metropolitan residents reported more satisfaction with family and close friends, while rural residents reported more satisfaction with the community and agricultural productivity. The authors explained this finding by suggesting that life satisfaction is maintained through compensation. That is, decreases in satisfaction in one domain are compensated by increases in satisfaction in another. Specifically, compensation occurs when an individual, who repeatedly experiences dissatisfaction in one life domain, allocates significant mental or physical resources from another life domain to make up for the satisfaction deficiency. In the preceding study, this was exemplified by rural residents who had fewer opportunities to socialize frequently with friends and family, however, compensated by gaining satisfaction from their community and the fruits of their agricultural labors.

In other words, individuals who feel dissatisfied in a life domain (Domain X) and allocate more mental and physical resources from that domain into another life domain (Domain Y) are likely to experience higher levels of life satisfaction overall than those who feel equally dissatisfied (in Domain X) but do not reallocate resources from there to another life domain (e.g., Domain Y). Allocating mental and physical resources in another life domain (Domain Y) serves to increase satisfaction in that domain (Domain Y) to compensate for the decrease in satisfaction in the original domain (Domain X). See Figure 8.1.

116

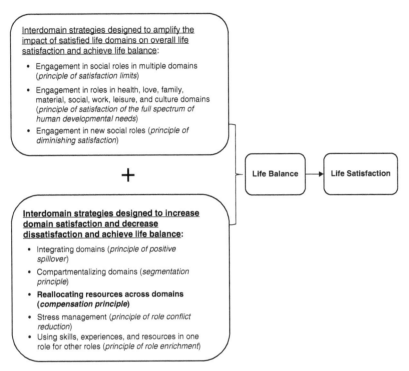

**Figure 8.1** Reallocating resources across domains (compensation principle)

## The Compensation Principle

Dissatisfaction in a salient life domain tends to decrease life satisfaction overall. This is because overall life satisfaction is strongly influenced by individual domain satisfaction. Hence, decreases in satisfaction in one domain are likely to decrease overall life satisfaction (Brief et al., 1993; Freund & Baltes, 2002; Judge et al., 2001; Tait et al., 1989). For example, decreases in satisfaction in work life are likely to decrease satisfaction with life overall. And decreases in overall life satisfaction are very troubling. People do what it takes to prevent significant decreases in overall life satisfaction. They may do this by reallocating resources across domains to ensure that decreases in satisfaction in an important domain can be compensated with increases in satisfaction in another domain. Doing so serves to maintain the level of overall life satisfaction that the person has adapted to. The key point here is compensation – or trading off decreases in satisfaction in one domain for increases in satisfaction in another.

How do researchers provide empirical evidence for the compensation effect? Is there a direct measure of capturing compensation? The answer is no. Researchers have pointed to an inverse (or negative) relationship between satisfaction in two life domains (e.g., the greater satisfaction with work life and the less satisfaction with leisure life, and vice versa) as evidence of the use of compensation (Rain, Lane, & Steiner, 1991). In other words, according to the compensation principle, there should be an inverse relationship between satisfaction in competing domains (e.g., work and family). The individual attempts to satisfy voids from one domain with satisfactions from the other (Clark, 2000).

Consider the following study conducted by Kabanoff and O'Brien (1982). They captured the work and leisure activities of 1,383 employed persons in a survey using five task attributes (influence, variety, pressure, skill utilization, and interaction) to test the compensation principle between work and leisure. The study revealed that high-status occupations (such as a physician or business owner) showed significant decreases in attributes such as influence, variety, and skill utilization from work to leisure. That is, high-status employees experience high levels of influence, variety, and skill utilization in their work life but fail to experience the same positive benefits in their leisure life. This finding applies only to high-status employees, not those with low status (such as janitor or hospital orderly).

The compensation principle can best be understood using the language of *homeostatically protected mood* (HPMood; see Capic, Li, & Cummins, 2018; Cummins, 2010, 2017; Cummins et al., 2018). The concept of HPMood refers to the notion that people have a baseline – or set point – for their normal level of life satisfaction. This set point is mostly stable and typically in the medium to positive range, for example, scoring 80 points on a 100-point rating scale (varying from low to high life satisfaction). The set point is not easily modifiable, and homeostatic forces are always at work to restore life satisfaction to its set point after an imbalance occurs. When life satisfaction is at a constant level, emotions are the cause of shifts in the set point that trigger homeostatic forces to restore the status quo. Thus, affective experience normally oscillates around an individual's set point. Homeostatic forces regulate the system to ensure dissatisfaction in a life domain does not decrease subjective wellbeing as well as work to restore life satisfaction to the set point.

When a homeostatic imbalance occurs, a set of homeostatic buffers are activated in order to restore balance. These buffers involve unconscious defenses, namely behavior and cognitive defenses. Thus, positive or negative deviations from the set point tend to activate the buffers to restore homeostasis. These buffers tend to be activated more forcefully in response to negative than to positive deviations to the set point because negative affect is associated with threats against survival. Chronic negative deviations from the set point can overwhelm the buffers resulting in chronic negative homeostatic imbalance (i.e., psychopathological conditions such as depression). One of the buffers is compensation. That is, compensation is a form of either a cognitive – or behavior – defense designed to restore homeostatic balance in life satisfaction.

## Compensation Strategies

There are two compensation strategies that have been well researched in the work-life balance literature, namely value-based compensation and behavior-based compensation (Edwards & Rothbard, 2000). See Table 8.1.

### Value-Based Compensation

Life balance can also be achieved by optimizing domain satisfaction by mentally changing domain salience. Consider the following scenario: Person A is satisfied with family life (+3 unit of satisfaction units on an 11-point scale varying from +5 to −5) but not satisfied with work life (−3 satisfaction units). Person A also believes that both family life and work life are equally important (0.8 importance points to each domain on a 1.0-point importance scale varying from "0" as "not important at all" to "1.0" as "extremely important"). Hence, family satisfaction is "+2.4" [(+3) × (0.8)] and work satisfaction is "−2.4" [(−3) × (0.8)]. Person B is also in the same boat – they feel happy with family life but unhappy with work life. Person B also believes that both domains are equally important. Note that in both cases, there is marked satisfaction in family life ("+2.4") and dissatisfaction in work life ("−2.4"). How do people manipulate the interplay between/among the domains to enhance life satisfaction overall?

Table 8.1 *Compensation strategies*

| Compensation strategy | Definition |
| --- | --- |
| Value-based strategy | Individuals reduce the importance ascribed to a negative role in a life domain to reduce the impact of domain dissatisfaction on overall life satisfaction. |
| Behavior-based strategy | Individuals invest more time and energy in an alternative role in another domain to generate domain satisfaction that serves to maintain overall life satisfaction. |

Person A makes a cognitive change by increasing the salience of family life – increasing importance weight from "0.8" to "1.0." This results in "+3.0" satisfaction points [(+3) × (1.0)] in family life. Decreasing the salience of work life – decreasing salience weight from "0.8" to "0.1" – results in "–0.3" satisfaction units [(–3) × (0.1)] in work life. That is, satisfaction in family life increases – from "+2.4" to "+3.0" [(+3) × (1.0)] – and dissatisfaction in work life decreases – from "–3.2" to "–0.3" [(–3) × (0.1)]. Meanwhile, person B makes no cognitive changes and remains the same. Thus, person A was able to increase satisfaction in family life and decrease dissatisfaction in work life through value-based compensation. Doing so serves to increase life satisfaction overall.

The theory of value-based compensation supports the research that has shown that there is a significant correlation between domain satisfaction and domain importance (Hsieh, 2003). That is, domains in which people express high levels of satisfaction are likely to be treated as more salient than domains with low satisfaction (or dissatisfaction). Consider the following study: Scott and Stumpf (1984) collected data on subjective wellbeing, domain satisfaction, and domain importance using a population of immigrants to Australia. The data clearly revealed a pattern of correlations in which most domain satisfaction scores were significantly correlated with their corresponding domain importance scores – friendship, material possessions, family recreation, and nation. Also consider research in social psychology showing that people report things they are not proficient at to be less important than the things that they are proficient at (e.g., Campbell, 1986; Harackiewicz, Sansone, & Manderlink, 1985; Lewicki, 1984; Rosenberg, 1979). These findings are also in line with the positive correlations between domain satisfaction and domain importance. These correlations mean that people tend to assign greater importance to life domains they feel satisfied with; and conversely, they assign low importance to domains they feel less satisfied with. This is the essence of value-based compensation.

To reiterate, value-based compensation reflects an association between domain satisfaction and domain salience. People increase the salience of domains they feel satisfied in and decrease the salience of domains they feel dissatisfied in. Why? They do so to increase life satisfaction – or at least prevent life satisfaction from falling below an acceptable level (Sirgy, 2002). Wu (2009) attempted to capture the value-based compensation effect by developing an index that reflects the correlation between have-want discrepancy scores from 12 different life domains and perceived importance scores of these domains – a correlation coefficient at the individual level. Individuals who engage in compensation are those who perceive life domains with high satisfaction to be more important than others. Wu calls this compensation phenomenon the "shifting tendency." Correlations between the *shifting tendency* and life satisfaction (as well as domain satisfaction scores) were positive, suggesting that the shifting tendency may be a strategy that enhances subjective wellbeing.

Consider the study by Shane and Heckhausen (2016) on adaptive lifespan development. The study, based on a large social survey of US adults (the Midlife in the United States National Longitudinal Study of Health and Well-Being – MIDUS I and II), indicated that individuals' domain-specific role engagement is positively related to their domain-specific situation quality and perceived control. That is, individuals place greater importance on goals in domains in which they have an established record of success and goal attainment.

In sum, the preceding discussion can be captured as follows: Individuals increase domain satisfaction by increasing salience of satisfied domains; and conversely, they decrease domain dissatisfaction by decreasing salience of dissatisfied domains. Overall life satisfaction is increased by doing so.

## Behavior-Based Compensation

Consider the following scenario: Person A is becoming increasingly unhappy with family life – satisfaction in family life drops from

+3 units to –2 units. This drop in satisfaction in family life is likely to adversely influence their life satisfaction overall. Person B is similarly unhappy with family life – satisfaction drops from +3 units to –2 units as well. Person A becomes more engaged at work by taking on more responsibility, socializing with his/her coworkers, and getting more recognition from his/her boss. That is, his/her satisfaction in work life jumps from a mere +1 units of satisfaction to +4 – a whopping increase of +3 units. This increase of satisfaction in work life serves to offset the decrease of satisfaction in family life. Person B does not do anything about his/her family situation (–2) nor work to increase satisfaction in any other domains. Ultimately, person A's life satisfaction is maintained, while person B's life satisfaction drops significantly.

Many seminal studies in work-life balance have documented the fact that involvement at work is inversely correlated with involvement in nonwork (e.g., Cotgrove, 1965; Clark, Nye, & Gecas, 1978; Fogarty, Rapoport, & Rapoport, 1971; Goldstein & Eichhorn, 1961; Haavio-Mannila, 1971; Haller & Rosenmayr, 1971; Rapoport, Rapoport, & Thiessen, 1974; Shea, Spitz, & Zeller, 1970; Walker & Woods, 1976). That is, the greater the involvement in work life, the less involvement in nonwork life. Other evidence suggests that individuals dissatisfied at work tend to increase their engagement in nonwork roles (e.g., Furnham, 1991; Shepard, 1974; Staines, 1980). For example, individuals in low-status jobs often feel dissatisfied with their jobs. To compensate for this dissatisfaction, they become more involved in leisure activities (Miller & Weiss, 1982). For example, they take significant pleasure and place great importance on winning prizes in a leisure activity, such as organized league bowling.

Also, consider the research on materialism. There is much evidence to suggest that materialism (strength of financial aspirations) is negatively related to subjective wellbeing (see literature review by Richins & Rudmin, 1994; Roberts & Clement, 2007). That is, those who score highly on measures of materialism report lower levels of subjective wellbeing, and vice versa (e.g., Ahuvia & Wong, 2002; Kasser & Ryan, 1993; Richins & Dawson, 1992; Sirgy, 1998). One explanation provided by Diener and Biswas-Diener (2009) is the notion of "retail therapy." Those who do not have close friends and other social resources tend to *compensate* by shopping. In other words, shopping becomes therapeutic and is a way of engaging in behavior-based compensation.

Finally, we can further refine the behavior-based compensation strategy by breaking it down into two tactics, namely supplemental and reactive (Zedeck, 1992; Zedeck & Mosier, 1990). An individual may engage in supplemental compensation when positive experiences are insufficient in one life domain (e.g., work life); and because they are insufficient, positive experiences are, therefore, pursued in another domain (e.g., family life). By contrast, reactive compensation occurs when the individual harbors negative experiences in one domain (e.g., work life). To deal with the dip in life satisfaction (consequence of the increase in dissatisfaction in the aforementioned domain), the individual makes up for this deficit by pursuing positive experiences in another domain (e.g., family life).

## Conditions Favorable to Compensation

In this section, I will point to certain conditions most likely to influence how people go about using the compensation strategy. These conditions are discussed in terms of situational, personal, and societal factors. See Table 8.2.

### *Situational Conditions*

The obvious situation that leads an individual to use a compensation strategy is repeated failure in a specific domain. For example, Matt is a teenage boy who loves soccer and decides to learn to play. Through repeated attempts, he finds himself unable to do well. He can't manipulate the ball; he can't seem to score; his soccer mates have admonished him for not passing the ball and losing control of the ball to the competition; his friends mocked his soccer ability; etc. What does he do to deal with his dissatisfaction with this aspect of his life? He withdraws from soccer. But withdrawing is not enough to compensate for the satisfaction deficit he experienced. To compensate for the loss of satisfaction and to protect the set point of his overall life satisfaction, he does one of the two things. He engages in value-based compensation by convincing himself that soccer is a "silly sport"; soccer is not important compared to other areas of his life; that his love life deserves much more attention and his resources should be diverted as such; and so on. Or he may engage in behavior-based compensation by choosing to channel his energies into another activity, such as playing music. He discovers

Table 8.2 *Conditions favorable to the use of compensation*

| Compensation strategy | Variables |
| --- | --- |
| Situational conditions | Repeated failure in specific roles in a life domain |
| Personal conditions | Self-perceptions of competency in specific roles in a life domain; stage in life |
| Societal conditions | Cultural congruence |

that he has a talent for composing songs; his friend just told him that a local band is looking for a songwriter. Channeling his resources in that direction may elevate his satisfaction in his leisure domain, which in turn may help him restore homeostatic balance in subjective wellbeing.

Of course, these value- and behavior-based compensation strategies are further facilitated by a host of other situational factors. Matt's friends may further encourage him to make the switch to music. Perhaps his parents may further support this decision. The music teacher endorses this decision.

## Personal Conditions

Life goals and goal selection in compensation can vary a great deal as a direct function of personal characteristics. For example, Matt's decision to shift his focus away from playing soccer to music composition instead is highly dependent on his perception of his own talent and skill in music composition. This self-perception is, of course, a personal characteristic and is most likely to impact his decision to shift focus. Besides self-concept, there may be a host of other personal characteristics that may impinge on the compensation decision. There may be personality factors, values, motives, lifestyle, interests, opinions, attitudes, and life stage characteristics at play.

Let's look a little more closely at the latter – life-stage characteristics. Life-stage characteristics are life goals prioritized as a function of the family life cycle. That is, different goals are treated as more important as a direct function of the individual's age. Consider the study by Shane and Heckhausen (2016) we discussed in the preceding section. That study was based on a large social survey of US adults (the Midlife in the United States National Longitudinal Study of Health and Well-Being – MIDUS I and II). The study showed that individuals'

engagement within the domains of work, health, and family relationships follow general trajectories across adulthood. In the young and
mid-adulthood stage of the lifespan, greater importance is placed on
work and relationships; however, priorities shift to focus on health
and relationships with family in late adulthood. Meaning that the life
stage should be considered one of the many possible personal conditions that affect value- and behavior-based compensation strategies.

## Societal Conditions

Changing life goals (mentally or physically) requires cultural congruence. That is, there is a host of societal norms related to what is
perceived as acceptable for certain demographics to engage in certain
types of activities. For example, in countries that have strict gender
roles, girls and women are restricted to shifting their energies only to
activities considered acceptable for their gender. A girl in an Islamic
country wanting to channel her energies to playing a sport like a soccer would be considered taboo. However, channeling her energies into
culturally congruent activities (e.g., sewing, singing, painting, or playing a musical instrument) would be encouraged. Societal conditions
reflect societal norms and operate as such.

## Summary and Conclusion

In this chapter, I described how people achieve a certain degree of
life balance by using compensation – reallocating resources from one life
domain to another. That is, individuals who feel dissatisfied in one life
domain (Domain X) and allocate more mental and physical resources
away from that domain and into another life domain (Domain Y) are
likely to experience higher levels of life satisfaction than those who feel
equally dissatisfied (in Domain X) but do not reallocate resources to
another life domain (e.g., Domain Y). Allocating mental and physical
resources in another life domain (Domain Y) serves to increase satisfaction in that domain (Domain Y) to compensate for the decrease in
satisfaction in the original domain (Domain X).

There are two compensation strategies that have been well
researched in the work-life balance literature, namely value-based
compensation and behavior-based compensation. Value-based compensation occurs when the individual reduces the importance ascribed

to a less-rewarding role in a life domain to reduce the impact of domain dissatisfaction on overall life satisfaction. By contrast, behavior-based compensation is when the individual invests more time and energy in an alternative (more satisfying) role in another domain to generate domain satisfaction that serves to maintain overall life satisfaction.

Finally, I described certain conditions most likely to influence how people apply the compensation strategy. Situational conditions involve a repeated failure in specific roles in a life domain. Personal conditions involve self-perceptions of competency in specific roles in a life domain as well as the individual's stage in life. Societal conditions involve cultural congruence.

# 9 | *Reducing Role Conflict*

The compensatory model of life satisfaction does not consider the interaction of roles between life domains. Remember the compensatory model and how it was described? The model is simple; it states that overall life satisfaction is nothing more than the sum of satisfaction units experienced in various life domains. Consider the following scenario: Carol experiences a moderate level of satisfaction in both work life and family life (e.g., +3 units of satisfaction in each domain on an 11-point scale varying from +5 to –5). However, she experiences conflict between roles in work life and family life (e.g., family demand interferes with work demand, and vice versa). In contrast, Ann experiences the same levels of domain satisfaction in both work life and family life (+3 units of satisfaction in each); however, Ann does not experience role conflict. The compensatory model of life satisfaction would predict that both individuals are likely to experience the same level of life satisfaction because both domains – work and family – are equally satisfied. However, life balance dictates that role conflict be accounted for in the way domain satisfaction contributes to life satisfaction. By taking into account role conflict, we come to the conclusion that Ann should experience higher levels of life satisfaction than Carol.

What is role conflict? Social scientists traditionally define this concept as when "role pressures associated with membership in one organization are in conflict with pressures stemming from membership in other groups" (Kahn et al., 1964, p. 20). That is, the demands of one role make the performance of another role more difficult (Katz & Kahn, 1978). In the context of work- and family-related roles, this means that role demand in work life and family life become incompatible to the degree that participation in work life is made more difficult by virtue of participation in family life, and vice versa (Greenhaus & Beutell, 1985). What do we mean by *role demand*? Role demand involves the responsibilities, requirements, expectations, duties, and commitments associated with a designated role such as family-, work-, friend-, church-, and neighbor-related roles.

One of the most significant aspects inherent in role conflict is difficulty balancing behaviors involved in multiple roles because of the shackles associated with traditional gender-role expectations (Napholz, 2000). Especially true in traditional cultures, women often feel – or are – responsible for everyone and everything related to the family. Consider the following quote by a woman who participated in a study on role conflict:

Women don't realize.... They're so busy taking care of everybody else's business and they're forgetting their own business and peace of mind. (Napholz, 2000, p. 259)

As a result, perceived – whether this is internal or external – failure to attend to family needs can cause an immense sense of guilt. Mothers who work outside of the home often face even greater challenges related to role conflict and associated feelings of guilt.

Oh, I need to do this thing. I have to do this thing. If I don't do this thing, I'm going to feel guilty, and as I'm doing it, sometimes that feeling will go with me as I'm doing it and I'll wind up burning the dinner. (Napholz, 2000, p. 260)

To better understand role conflict and how it plays a key role in life balance, consider how work-life balance researchers measure work–family conflict. Professors Richard Netemeyer, James Boles, and Robert McMurrian (Netemeyer, Boles, & McMurrian, 1996) have developed work–family conflict and family–work conflict scales that are now well established in the work-life balance literature. See survey items in Table 9.1. These scales were validated by negative (i.e., inverse) correlations – one variable increases while the other decreases – between role conflict (both work–family conflict and family–work conflict) and on-job constructs (such as organizational commitment, job satisfaction, self-efficacy, and sales performance) and off-job constructs (such as life satisfaction and satisfaction with the marital relationship). That is, those who experienced high levels of role conflict also reported low levels of organizational commitment (little-to-no loyalty to the firm), job satisfaction (unhappy with one's job and work situation), self-efficacy (lack of self-confidence in one's ability to get the job done right), and sales performance (poor sales).

**Table 9.1** *Work–family and family–work conflict measures*

*Work–Family Conflict Scale*
1. The demands of my work interfere with my home and family life.
2. The amount of time my job takes up makes it difficult to fulfill family responsibilities.
3. Things I want to do at home do not get done because of the demands my job puts on me.
4. My job produces strain that makes it difficult to fulfill family duties.
5. Due to work-related duties, I have to make changes in my plans for family activities.

*Family–Work Conflict Scale*
1. The demands of my family or spouse/partner interfere with work-related activities.
2. I have to put off doing things at work because of demands on my time at home.
3. Things I want to do at work don't get done because of the demands of my family or spouse/partner.
4. My home life interferes with my responsibilities at work such as getting to work on time, accomplishing daily tasks, and working overtime.
5. Family-related strain interferes with my ability to perform job-related duties.

*Notes:* Responses are captured on a 5-point Likert-type scale (1 = strongly disagree to 5 = strongly agree).
*Source:* Adapted from Netemeyer, Boles, and McMurrian (1996, p. 410).

In addition, role conflict was positively correlated – both variables increase – with job tension, intention to leave the organization, search for another job, biological markers of ill-being, and depression. That is, those who experienced high levels of role conflict also reported that they are planning to quit the firm and searching for another job. They also scored highly on symptoms of physical ill-being such as lack of sleep and reported health problems, as well as measures of depression.

Research has shown that role conflict in life domains (those considered as important by an individual such as work life, family life, and social life) has an adverse effect on domain satisfaction and overall life satisfaction (e.g., Kossek & Ozeki, 1998). A high level of psychological involvement in one role is usually associated with increased amounts of time and involvement devoted to that role,

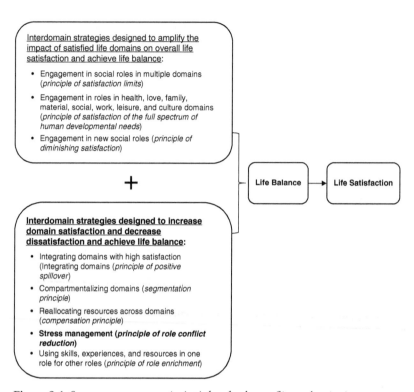

**Figure 9.1** Stress management (principle of role conflict reduction)

thereby making it difficult to deal with role demand in other life domains (e.g., Greenhaus & Beutell, 1985). Individuals experiencing role conflict across life domains are likely to experience stress, which in turn reduces overall life satisfaction (e.g., Frone, Russell, & Cooper, 1992). Why would they experience stress? To maintain successful performance in these conflicting roles, they must invest much more time and energy in those roles to maintain an acceptable level of life satisfaction. This allocation of more resources to maintain successful performance in conflicting social roles is most often accompanied by psychological stress commonly manifested in terms of general psychological strain, somatic/physical symptoms, depression, substance abuse, burnout, work-related stress, and family-related stress. Positive affectivity is negatively correlated with stress (e.g., Brief et al., 1993; Judge et al., 1998; Watson, 2000; Watson et al., 1988). See Figure 9.1.

Consider the following study by Knecht, Wiese, and Fruend (2016) – a three-wave longitudinal study spanning one year involving adult men and women. The study examined different forms of conflict between leisure life and the life domains of work and family in addition to their relation to subjective wellbeing. The study findings suggest that conflict between any of these three life domains is negatively related to concurrent subjective wellbeing (i.e., feelings of wellbeing experienced during the same time frame involving role conflict). That is, the study demonstrates that, similar to work–family conflict, conflict with the leisure domain can significantly decrease subjective wellbeing.

## The Principle of Role Conflict Reduction

Research has shown that life balance can be achieved when social roles in work and nonwork-life domains are compatible with minimal conflict (e.g., Greenhaus & Allen, 2011). That is, stress management is typically a suggested approach to deal with the stress generated by role conflict. Role conflict can take multiple forms including (Greenhaus & Beutell, 1985) time-, strain-, and behavior-based conflict. *Time-based conflict* refers to time pressures from one role preventing individuals from meeting expectations in another role or creating a preoccupation with one role while one is physically attempting to fulfill another role. For example, an individual may experience time-based conflict when the amount of time devoted to the work life interferes with performing family-related responsibilities. In other words, excessive time devoted to work-related tasks may make it difficult to carry out family responsibilities. *Strain-based conflict* occurs when tension, anxiety, and/or fatigue from one role affects performance in another role. For example, an individual may experience strain-based conflict when strain created by work responsibilities interferes with leisure, and vice versa. Strain may manifest in the form of irritability and anxiety. *Behavior-based conflict* occurs when in-role behavior from one role is incompatible with behaviors expected in another role. For example, an employee who schedules to meet a client that conflicts with a family vacation trip. The scheduling of both events is behavior-based, and both actions conflict with each other.

In sum, individuals who successfully manage stress stemming from role conflict are likely to experience higher life satisfaction than those who fail to manage that stress. Specifically, role conflict causes significant stress, which takes a toll on life satisfaction – stress stemming from time-based role conflict, strain-based role conflict, and behavior-based role conflict. Stress management to reduce time-based conflict, strain-based conflict, and behavior-based conflict serves to reduce domain dissatisfaction. In doing so, life satisfaction is maintained at acceptable adaptation levels.

## Stress Management Strategies

Stress management involves three distinct sets of techniques, techniques to reduce stress from (1) time-based conflict, (2) strain-based conflict, and (3) behavior-based conflict. See Table 9.2.

### Stress Management Related to Time-Based Conflict

To reiterate, time-based conflict occurs when time demands associated with participation in one role interfere with participation in another role (Greenhaus & Beutell, 1985). That is, problems arising from scheduling time between work and family roles is the essence of work–family conflict (Frone, Russell, & Cooper, 1992). Research has shown that proper time management can reduce work–family conflict (Adams & Jex, 1999). Three clusters of time good management behaviors have been identified, namely (1) setting goals and priorities, (2) engaging in the mechanics of time management such as making lists and schedules, and (3) having a preference for organization (Macan et al., 1990).

*Setting goals and priorities* is an important aspect of time management. Individuals who are good at setting goals and priorities would endorse such statements as, "I set short-term goals for what I want to accomplish in a few days or weeks," and "I set priorities to determine the order in which I will perform tasks each day" (Macan et al., 1990).

*Engaging in the mechanics of time management* involves things such as a good system for recording appointments with reminders, as well as making a list of things to do each day and checking off each task as it is completed (Macan et al., 1990). Of course, an important aspect of scheduling is being cognizant of scheduling conflicts. That is, one should avoid scheduling projects and events that may conflict with one another (Epstein & Kalleberg, 2004).

Table 9.2 *Stress management strategies*

| Type of stress management strategies | Examples |
|---|---|
| Strategies to reduce time-based conflict | Planning and scheduling tasks and events in ways that do not conflict. |
| Strategies to reduce strain-based conflict | Engaging in regular exercise, participating in wellness programs, meditation, praying, social support, challenging the belief system causing conflict, and cyberloafing. |
| Strategies to reduce behavior-based conflict | Identifying behaviors that may cause role conflict and taking action to refrain from engaging in those behaviors. |

Time management also involves a *preference for organization*. That is, carrying out tasks on time requires a minimal degree of organization. A messy and disorganized workplace and home may obstruct people from carrying out tasks on their to-do lists on time. As such, organization is important in time management.

Another challenge in time management training is *dealing with procrastination*. It is common for individuals to be habitually behind schedule on their personal projects – psychologists refer to these people as "trait procrastinators" (Lay & Schouwenburg, 1993). These individuals procrastinate for a variety of reasons. These can often include:

• Protection of self-esteem through self-handicapping (i.e., waiting to complete the project until very close to the deadline allows the individual to attribute poor performance on the project to "running out of time"; this attribution softens the blow of poor performance on one's self-esteem).

• Avoidance of aversive tasks (i.e., procrastinating is a way to avoid engaging and completing tasks that the person perceives as unpleasant, undesirable, and perhaps painful).

• Demonstration of autonomy (i.e., procrastination signals noncompliance or at least resistance to conformity, which in turn signals that the person is in control of their own surroundings).

• Avoidance of anxiety (i.e., procrastinating allows the person to put off the task in question to avoid the anxiety associated with the possibility of poor task performance).

- Response to their perfectionist tendencies (i.e., procrastinating is a way to cope with perfectionism; perfectionists anticipate "less than perfect" performance due to their high standards; as such, they procrastinate to avoid having to deal with the anxiety over the "less-than-perfect" performance).
- Lack self-regulation (i.e., some people procrastinate because they are not disciplined enough to monitor time and abide by a schedule).

A literature review of procrastination interventions (van Eerde & Klingsieck, 2018) categorized the interventions in terms of three programs, namely training self-regulatory skills, building self-efficacy, and organizing social support. The goal of *training of self-regulatory skills* is to establish good work habits that ultimately serve to prevent procrastination. The training techniques involve goal definition, setting deadlines, defining time slots, monitoring progress, and avoiding distractions. *Building self-efficacy* involves changing thinking patterns that lead to procrastination – changing negative and unproductive thoughts into positive and productive thoughts. *Organizing social support* involves sharing problems arising from procrastination with others. The support group helps address those problems and helps by working to collectively solve them. The support group also helps in recruiting others to monitor and remind the procrastinators of impending deadlines and encouraging the execution of the planned behavior. The support group also helps to reduce stress and anxiety related to procrastination.

## Stress Management Related to Strain-Based Conflict

Examples of stress management techniques designed to reduce strain-based conflict include activities designed to improve mental and physical health such as breathing exercises, meditation, physical exercise, social support, among many others. Research has shown that leaders (high-ranking executives) who *exercise regularly* have increased stamina and mental focus compared to those who do not exercise or who exercise less regularly (Leiter & Maslach, 2005; Neck & Cooper, 2000). Some research has shown that the unwillingness to exercise may be a consequence of role conflict – conflict between work and family roles does not leave the individual with enough time or energy (e.g., Allen & Armstrong, 2006; Grace et al., 2006; Grzywacz & Marks, 2001; Roos et al., 2007). In contrast, research has also shown that those who exercise report less work–family conflict. For example, a study conducted by Professor Russell Clayton and colleagues at Saint Leo University (Clayton et al., 2015) uses a sample of 476 working adults to examine exercise and work–family conflict. Their study was able to demonstrate that physical exercise (physical activity that is planned, structured, repetitive, and purposeful) has indirect effects on work–family conflict by increasing self-efficacy in managing work–family conflict and decreasing psychological strain. That is, the study findings suggest that physical exercise heightens one's belief that they can manage their work and family lives (i.e., self-efficacy), and as such, they can better cognitively manage work–family conflict.

*Wellness programs* have become fashionable in the corporate world, and physical fitness is now an entrenched and well-established program among other more traditional wellness programs (Kossek, Ozeki, & Kosier, 2001). Consider the following companies as an example. Both Zappos.com and Google were named in *Fortune*'s "100 Best Companies to Work For." Among other perks, both companies provide employees with onsite fitness programs (e.g., yoga classes). Considerable evidence has shown that wellness programs do make a positive impact on reducing absenteeism and health insurance premiums as well as increasing job satisfaction, employee morale, and employee retention (DeGroot & Kiker, 2003; Parks & Steelman, 2008).

How about *meditation*? Consider the following study by Kiburz, Allen, and French (2017). The study examined the effectiveness of a brief mindfulness-based training intervention that involved a one-hour workshop followed by 13 days of behavioral self-monitoring. The goal of the study was to reduce work–family conflict, and the intervention was successful in doing so. Specifically, those who participated in the intervention experienced greater mindfulness, less work-to-family conflict, and less family-to-work conflict than did those who did not participate in the intervention.

*Praying* can be considered a form of meditation. A study conducted on female, Muslim academicians in Malaysia (Achour, Grine, & Mohd Nor, 2014) found that many participants believed turning to religion in times of need is helpful in managing their stress. They asserted that they turn to "Allah" to help solve all problems related to family, work, and others. From this, it is clear that praying can be an effective strategy to deal with the high demand from multiple roles. Consider the following quotation from one of the study participants:

When I face any conflict, I have one strategy to cope: I turn to Allah, because I believe that only Allah can help me solve my problem. I also pray tahajjud (night prayers), make dua (supplications) because only Allah knows every-thing about me, my family, and my husband. He is the only One who can resolve our problem. (Muslim female academician #3, 45 years old, mother of five; Achour, Grine, & Mohd Nor, 2014; p. 1010)

Resources, such as *social support*, can also reduce work–family con-flict and minimize the detrimental effects of role conflict on health and wellbeing. Social support has been proven to have a beneficial impact on reducing psychological strain, increasing job and family satisfaction, and reducing work–family conflict (e.g., Byron, 2005; Drummond et al., 2017). The converse is also true – lack of social sup-port can exacerbate work–family conflict (Ayman & Antani, 2008), which in turn increases psychological strain and reduces satisfaction in both work life and family life. Social support is usually provided by a significant other or another substantial family relationship. A support ive partner is usually an important resource to reduce strains experi-enced in the family domain and alleviate family-to-work conflict (e.g., Frone et al., 1997; Greenhaus & Beutell, 1985; Voydanoff, 2005b). Given that family distress is associated with family-to-work conflict, a supportive partner acts as a buffer to reduce family distress. Consider the same study on Malaysian academics (Achour, Grine, & Mohd Nor, 2014). In addition to using religion as a coping strategy to deal with work–family conflict, the women also identified social support as a key strategy to deal with the demands involved with multiple roles.

Yet another strategy to reduce role conflict is to *challenge the belief system causing you to feel role conflict*. Most belief systems are indoctrinated in you from childhood. Especially prevalent and pervasive is the belief system surrounding sex and gender roles. Men are often taught that they are supposed to be the breadwinner in the family. They need to work hard in order to bring in financial resources to support family needs. In contrast, many women are told that they are responsible for the daily needs of the family inside the home. They are supposed to feed the family, clean house, play nurse, and play hostess in organizing social events, among other stereotypi-cal tasks. Challenging these gender role expectations is an effective way to reduce role conflict (Glazebrook & Munjas, 1986). It is more acceptable now than ever before for women to challenge gender role norms. Traditional concepts of masculinity and femininity have been obfuscated, and individuals can now choose to engage in behaviors without regard to gender role expectations with less fear of being ostracized. A woman may challenge the norm by saying something to this effect:

Just because I am a woman, I am expected to fix dinner and be the primary caregiver; I will not accept that. This is too old fashioned; it is too anti-quated; we live in a different era; both men and women must share respon-sibilities in the home and outside the home equally.

An interesting coping strategy that many people use at work to reduce stress is "cyberloafing." *Cyberloafing* refers to "any voluntary act of employees using their companies' internet access during office hours to surf nonwork-related websites for nonwork purposes and access" (Lim, Teo, & Loo, 2002, p. 67). Although cyberloafing has a negative connotation, researchers have discovered that this activity can have a positive effect on employees (Lim & Chen, 2012). Their study findings revealed that cyberloafing

- makes work more interesting;
- provides cognitive support to deal with work and nonwork-related problems;
- makes employees more well versed and interesting, allows relief from work;
- motivates employees to perform better; and
- allows employees to take an innocuous break from a stressful environment.

## Stress Management Related to Behavior-Based Conflict

An example of a stress management technique that can assist in reduc-ing behavior-based conflict is to become more conscious of behaviors that may cause role conflict and to take action to refrain from engag-ing in those behaviors in ways to avoid role conflict.

We need to realize that we all engage in a multitude of both good and bad behaviors on a daily basis. Some of these behaviors may conflict with one another causing us to feel more satisfied in a certain life domain while usurping satisfaction from another domain. Take the simple exam-ple of working on a project through lunch. You usually eat a healthy lunch made up of a good tuna salad with soup. Working through lunch forces you to snack on candy and other junk food instead. Yet working through lunch may have helped complete a project on time. This means that this behavior enhanced role performance in the work domain, which has contributed to increased satisfaction in work life. However, snacking on junk food made you gain an extra few pounds, which made you feel unhappy about your weight gain. Furthermore, you are diabetic, which means that you need to regulate your food intake, especially foods with high sugar and salt content. As such, you feel bad about your health. One avenue to reducing stress related to behavior-based conflict can be achieved by learning to become cognizant of conflicting behaviors – those that may lead to satisfaction in one domain while producing dissatisfaction in another domain.

Another way to reduce stress arising from behavior-based conflict is to learn to say no to demands so that you can take care of yourself. Consider the following quote from another participant in the Malaysian academic study.

Addictive relationships are not only with partners but with kids. It's waking me up. Now, I'm kicking ass. A few weeks ago, my brother called me for a ride, and I said, "no. I live on the north side and you want me to come all the way over to the south side? No." My mom gets on the phone, "Well, are you taking Steve?" "No," [I said]. "Did you tell him?" "yes, I did." [I said]. That's another thing; you don't tell a man no when it's your brother or your son, or what, and they are always supposed to come first. That's the way I was always taught. (Napholz, 2000, p. 260)

## Conditions Favorable to Stress Management

Comparable to the preceding chapters, I will discuss those conditions favorable to role conflict reduction strategies in terms of three sets of factors: situational, personal, and societal. See Table 9.3.

### Situational Conditions

When should anyone apply any single or combination of the stress management techniques – stress management techniques related to time-, strain-, and behavior-based conflict? The obvious answer is when the situation calls for it. That is, applying the stress management techniques in situations in which there is low work-life conflict is unwarranted and determining when they are necessary is highly subjective dependent on circumstances.

Table 9.3 *Conditions favorable to stress management strategies*

| Conditions category | Variables |
|---|---|
| Situational conditions | Situations in which meeting role demand in a particular life domain that interferes with meeting role demand in another domain. |
| Personal conditions | Individuals with low self-efficacy. |
| Societal conditions | Societies stricken by disaster; increased telecommuting. |

## Personal Conditions

The stress management techniques previously described (stress management based on time-, strain-, and behavior-based conflict) can best be used by individuals who are low on *self-efficacy*. Self-efficacy refers to how an individual believes in his/her ability to complete tasks. Those high in self-efficacy tend to have high confidence in the way they can solve problems and get things done (e.g., Butler, Gasser, & Smart, 2004). Several researchers have investigated the effects of *self-efficacy* on work–family conflict (e.g., Erdwins et al., 2001; Ozer, 1995). These researchers were able to empirically demonstrate that women's self-efficacy in both family and work domains can help mitigate work–family conflict. Specifically, women who reported higher confidence in their ability as a parent and worker also reported being less overwhelmed by the demands stemming from their multiple roles – which in turn plays a significant role in reducing work–family conflict and enhancing subjective wellbeing. It should be noted that although this study focused on women, the study findings may be generalizable to both men and women.

Researchers have developed measures of multiple role self-efficacy (i.e., perceived ability to manage more than one role) and more specifically, work–family self-efficacy (i.e., perceived ability to effectively handle responsibilities in both family life and work life) (e.g., Butler, Gasser, & Smart, 2004; Johnson, 2003). For example, Johnson (2003) found that as multiple role in self-efficacy increased, work–family conflict decreased. Along the same vein, Butler et al. (2004) were able to demonstrate that work–family self-efficacy is positively related to greater use of resources – resources that help mitigate work–family conflict. Perrone and Civiletto (2004) found that the relationship between role strain and life satisfaction was mediated by self-efficacy. More specifically, individuals experiencing high role strain, who had high coping efficacy, were reported to be more satisfied with life, compared to individuals with high role strain and low coping efficacy.

The research on the relationship between self-efficacy and work–family conflict indicates that *enhancing self-efficacy* can be a strategy to allow individuals to be fully engaged in multiple roles with little work–family conflict and greater wellbeing. Slan-Jerusalim and Chen (2009) provided counseling advice about self-efficacy. The counselor can measure the client's self-efficacy in both the work and family roles. Example questions: (1) "How do you feel about your ability to manage your staff effectively?" (work self-efficacy); (2) "How do you feel about your ability to be a loving mother?" (family self-efficacy); and (3) "How do you feel about your ability to juggle your work and family demands?" (multiple role self-efficacy or work–family self-efficacy). The goal in measuring self-efficacy is to enhance the client's awareness of their self efficacy in the context of both work life and family life. The counselor could then focus on guiding the client to develop competency in areas the client admits deficiencies. Thus, counseling could help develop coping skills to effectively manage work-life conflict. These coping skills can be the suggested stress management techniques we discussed earlier (i.e., stress management based on time-, strain-, and behavior-based conflict).

## Societal Conditions

There are many macrolevel situations that may call for the increased use of stress management techniques. Consider the recent incidence of the COVID-19 pandemic. Governments worldwide mandated social distancing, which prompted most workplaces to switch to telecommuting (i.e., work remotely from home). Working from home can be effective for some people but not for others. Prepandemic society was structured to benefit people who engaged in work outside the home in places such as office buildings, plants, stores, and other work-like facilities. For most, home was the family sanctuary. Hence, society encouraged the separation of work life from nonwork life. We discussed this social phenomenon in detail in terms of "segmentation" (Chapter 7). As such, societal conditions that force people to telecommute may cause work-life conflict; and as such, those conditions call for the use of stress management.

## Summary and Conclusion

Role conflict refers to demand in one role in a particular life domain that leads to behavior to meet that role demand in ways that interfere with meeting role demand in other life domains. In the context of work- and family-related roles, this means that role responsibilities in work life and family life become incompatible to the degree that participation in work life is made more difficult by virtue of participation in family life, and vice versa.

Individuals who successfully manage stress stemming from role conflict are likely to experience higher life satisfaction than those who fail to manage that stress. Specifically, role conflict causes significant stress, which negatively impacts life satisfaction – stress stemming from time-based role conflict, strain-based role conflict, and behavior-based role conflict. Stress management to reduce time-based conflict, strain-based conflict, and behavior-based conflict serves to reduce domain dissatisfaction. In doing so, life satisfaction is maintained at acceptable adaptation levels.

Strategies to reduce time-based conflict involve planning and scheduling tasks and events in ways that do not conflict and deal with procrastination. Strategies to reduce strain-based conflict involve activities such as engaging in regular exercises, participation in wellness programs, meditation, praying, social support, challenging the established belief system, and cyberloafing. Strategies to reduce behavior-based conflict involve the identification of behaviors that may cause role conflict and taking action to refrain from engaging in those behaviors.

I then discussed conditions favorable to role conflict reduction strategies in terms of three sets of factors: situational, personal, and societal. Situational conditions involve situations in which meeting role demand in a particular life domain that interferes with meeting role demand in another domain. Personal conditions involve the concept of self-efficacy. Finally, societal conditions involve major disasters that may strike major geographic regions and increased telecommuting.

# 10 | *Using Skills, Experiences, and Resources in One Role for Other Roles*

Consider the following scenario: A worker experiences imbalance in domain satisfaction between work life and family life. That is, their satisfaction at work is +4 units – on a 11-point satisfaction scale, varying from –5 (very dissatisfied) to +5 (very satisfied). Recently, their satisfaction in family life was +3 but has now plummeted to –2 (moderate degree of dissatisfaction in family life). That is, their satisfaction in family life has decreased significantly, but their satisfaction at work remained constant. They are experiencing this diminished satisfaction in family life due to conflict with their adolescent children. The worker remembers using conflict resolution strategies at work that were successful in resolving conflict with members of their project team at work. The worker applies the same conflict resolution strategies at home to deal with the family conflict – with positive results. Doing so managed to change the satisfaction in family life from a –2 back to a +3. The increase in family life satisfaction ultimately helped maintain an acceptable level of overall life satisfaction.

There are situations in which people use skills, experiences, and resources in one role for other roles to enhance balanced satisfaction among life domains. In other words, resources in one role can improve or further enhance performance and satisfaction in another role – referred to as *role enrichment*. For example, work-to-family enrichment occurs when work experiences or knowledge serve to increase satisfaction in family life; and similarly, family-to-work enrichment occurs when family experiences or knowledge contributes to heightened satisfaction in work life (e.g., Greenhaus & Powell, 2006; Voydanoff, 2004). Doing so helps workers enhance domain satisfaction. That is, learning that occurs in one life domain is easily transferred to other life domains allowing the individual to generate more domain satisfaction through role engagement and goal attainment. See Figure 10.1.

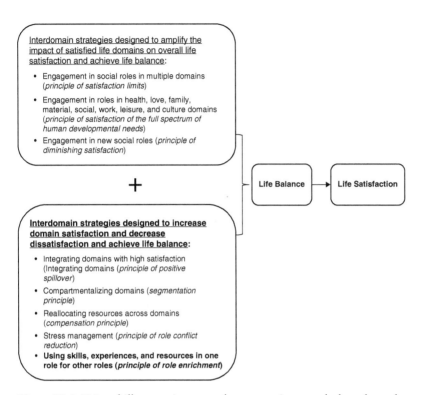

Figure 10.1 Using skills, experiences, and resources in one role for other roles (principle of role enrichment)

## The Principle of Role Enrichment

Research has documented the effect of *role enrichment* on overall life satisfaction when the two roles are integrated (e.g., Olson-Buchanan & Boswell, 2006), when the skills and resource requirements are similar (e.g., Greenhaus & Powell, 2006), or when role performance in one life domain becomes increasingly interdependent with another (e.g., Hanson & Hammer, 2006; Ilies et al., 2009). Elevated levels of role enrichment serve to improve role performance in work and nonwork domains, which in turn contributes to balanced domain satisfaction. That is, skills, psychological resources, and material resources generated in a life domain can be applied to roles in other life domains to increase role performance in those domains (e.g., Hanson & Hammer, 2006). Furthermore, individuals with high role enrichment are less likely to experience stress and anxiety from increased role demand.

Table 10.1 *Survey items measuring role enrichment between school life and family life*

- Being a student has made me a better parent.
- Being a parent has made me a better student.
- Being a student and a parent at the same time has made me happier than if I were only one or the other.
- Being a student and a parent at the same time has made me more responsible than if I were only one or the other.

*Source:* Westring & Ryan (2010).

Such individuals apply their skills and resources across social roles, producing more positive outcomes – less psychological distress and anxiety in performing multiple roles and a heightened sense of self-efficacy in those roles (Wiese et al., 2010).

Role enrichment may involve a variety of work and nonwork domains. To appreciate the concept of role enrichment, let's examine how social scientists measure the concept. Here is an example metric from the work-life balance research literature regarding work-to-family and family-to-work facilitation (Van Steenbergen, Ellemers, & Mooijaart, 2007), referred to as a "Work–Family Facilitation" scale. A sample work-to-family facilitation item is "Because of my work, I am more able to put home-related matters into perspective," and a sample family-to-work facilitation item is "Because of my home life, I am more able to put work-related problems aside." Table 10.1 shows survey items of role enrichment in relation to graduate students.

How does role enrichment improve life balance and enhance overall life satisfaction? A multitude of research exists that examines how role enrichment – as well as other mechanisms such as "resource enrichment," "positive spillover," "role facilitation," and "role enhancement" – improves life satisfaction (Greenhaus & Powell, 2006). Work-life balance researchers suggest that positive experiences in one role can produce positive experiences in another role through at least one mechanism. Specifically, participation in some roles creates skills and resources that can be applied in other roles. Resources generated in a specific role are used to enhance role performance. Role performance leads to increased positive affect in that role. Increased positive affect in that role may lead to increased performance in another role, which in turn leads to increased positive affect in the original role. As such, increased positive affect in both roles leads to increased life satisfaction. For example, management skills learned on how to communicate with workers are implemented to enhance job performance, which leads to increased job satisfaction. Communication skills learned at work to communicate with subordinates are implemented to enhance job performance. Those same skills help increase efficient and open communication at home, which leads to fewer conflicts and increased family satisfaction. Increased satisfaction in work life and family life then contributes to increased satisfaction in life overall.

We can succinctly capture the preceding discussion as follows: Individuals who use their skills, experiences, and resources in one role for other roles across life domains are likely to experience greater domain satisfaction (in dissatisfied domains) than those who do not. That is, they use skills, experiences, and resources in one domain to increase satisfaction in another domain (or mitigate decreases in satisfaction in another domain) and doing so helps to increase (or preserve) life satisfaction overall.

## Role Enrichment Strategies

There are at least four strategies that characterize role enrichment. These are (1) skills, (2) perspectives, (3) flexibility, and (4) resources – physical, psychological, social, and material (Greenhaus & Powell, 2006). See Table 10.2.

### Skills

Skills refer to a broad set of task-related cognitive abilities including – but not limited to – people skills, coping skills, multitasking skills, and knowledge and wisdom derived from past experiences in specific roles (Greenhaus & Powell, 2006). These skills can be generalized to be used across various roles in different life domains. That is, those skills that have proven successful in meeting role demand in one domain are used in another domain to meet role demand in another domain. Doing so improves role performance in the other domain leading to increased satisfaction in that domain. For example, a salesperson has built strong people skills over the years in their line of work: listening, communicating, negotiating, and persuading retail customers. These people skills are then applied to family life by improvements in listening,

Table 10.2 *Role enrichment strategies*

| Role enrichment strategies | Definition |
| --- | --- |
| Skills | The use of skills (people skills, time management skills, multitasking skills, etc.) often used in one domain to improve role performance can also be used to improve role performance and increase satisfaction in another domain. |
| Perspectives | Adopting a perspective (understanding personality differences, valuing cultural diversity, appreciating another person's position on issues, valuing trust, etc.) often used in one domain to improve role performance can also be used to improve role performance and increase satisfaction in another domain. |
| Flexibility | Applying rules of flexibility (i.e., discretion to determine the timing, pace, and location at which role demand is met) often used in one domain to improve role performance can also be used to improve role performance and increase satisfaction in another domain. |
| Resources | Applying resources (i.e., psychological, physical, social, and material resources) often used in one domain to improve role performance can also be used to improve role performance and increase satisfaction in another domain. |

communicating, negotiating, and persuading other family members. Improvements in family life mean increased satisfaction in family life, which in turn contributes to increased satisfaction in life overall.

## Perspectives

Perspectives involve ways of perceiving situations, such as understanding personality differences, valuing cultural diversity, adopting another person's perspective to better understand and appreciate their position on things, and valuing trust – understanding that we can all do better by trusting others as well as trusting institutions (Greenhaus & Powell, 2006). Adopting a particular perspective often used in one domain that has proven successful in meeting role demand and improving role performance can be used in another domain to do the same – improve role performance and increase satisfaction. For example, a manager learns that trusting their subordinates by allowing them to participate in decision-making, delegating authority, and encouraging them to do the job using their own means and methods can also be applied to their children. By allowing them to choose what chores they want to do and further allowing them to do them in the way they see fit, rather than showing a lack of trust by micromanaging. As such, adopting an attitude that focuses on accountability in managing the workplace can also produce positive results in family life, which in turn should increase personal happiness.

## Flexibility

Flexibility refers to the discretion to determine the timing, pace, and location at which role demand is met. This has been recognized often in the work–family literature as a means to help achieve work-life balance (Greenhaus & Powell, 2006). Applying rules of flexibility often used in one domain (rules that produced rewarding experiences in that domain) can be used in another domain to do the same – improve role performance and increase satisfaction. Consider the same manager from the previous example. They learn that flexibility in the workplace can produce positive job performance results. That is, allowing subordinates to choose their job parameters can make them more productive: selecting when, where, and how fast to work on what task. The same flexibility principle can enhance household work – household chores such as cleaning, cooking, shopping, chauffeuring, entertaining, and so on. Allow family members more flexibility in completing household chores. Doing so could ensure that the household chores are done with better results and as such contributes to family satisfaction.

## Resources

People use all types of resources to enhance performance in specific roles: including psychological, physical, social, and material resources (Greenhaus & Powell, 2006). One can use similar resources applied in the context of a specific role in a given domain to another role in another domain – resources that led to successful performance in the original role. Doing so serves to increase satisfaction in the other domain. Psychological resources may involve cognitive and emotional strengths such as self-efficacy, self-esteem, optimism, and hope. Physical resources involve physical health and capacity. Social resources involve the goodwill that is present in social relationships. Material resources include things like money and gifts. Consider the latter, material resources. A manager finds that Christmas bonus for employees contributes to their overall trust and goodwill in the company, which in turn contributes to employee productivity and job satisfaction. Using the same concept, the manager provides Christmas gifts to their significant other and children that also serve to enhance goodwill and morale within the family.

### Conditions Favorable to Role Enrichment Strategies

Comparable to the preceding chapters, I will discuss those conditions favorable to role enrichment strategies in terms of three sets of factors: situational, personal, and societal. See Table 10.3.

### *Situational Conditions*

There are many situations that may invoke the use of role enrichment strategies. Situations in various life domains may present problems (i.e., increases in role demand). To solve these problems (and meet role demand), the individual could tap into strengths they may have in the context of other domains. For example, problems communicating between spouses are common – I get defensive every time my spouse criticizes things I do around the house. Employing a role enrichment strategy, I recall what I usually do in the workplace. I know that I communicate very well with my coworkers and my supervisor, even when they criticize me. To do so, I remain objective and don't allow my emotions to run away with me. Can I do the same at home? Can I step away and process my spouse's criticisms objectively, without feeling that her comments are "personal attacks" on my integrity? Learning to do the same at home so is the goal of role enrichment. As such, consider this as an example of a situational condition that warrants the application of a role enrichment strategy.

Table 10.3 *Conditions favorable to role enrichment strategies*

| Conditions category | Variables |
|---|---|
| Situational conditions | Increased role demand in a particular life domain |
| Personal conditions | Individuals high in core self-evaluations |
| Societal conditions | Increased educational and training opportunities |

## Personal Conditions

Some people are much better at applying role enrichment strategies than others. This may have something to do with their personality. One such personality trait is core self-evaluations. Let's examine the research. Core self-evaluation is a personality concept that reflects a positive self-image (Judge et al., 1998). This concept has several dimensions, namely self-esteem, generalized self-efficacy, locus of control, and neuroticism. That is, individuals high on core self-evaluations tend to have high self-esteem, perceive themselves as having the ability to engage in a variety of tasks and complete them successfully, believe that they have control over their environment, and are well adjusted with low levels of anxiety. A sample measurement item of core self-evaluations reads, "I am confident that I get the success I deserve in life" (responses are captured using a 12-point scale varying from "strongly disagree" to "strongly agree") (Judge et al., 2003). Evidence suggests that workers with more positive core self-evaluations tend to experience higher levels of role enrichment compared to those with negative core self-evaluations (Westring & Ryan, 2010). This means that individuals with high core self-evaluations are in a better position to improve balance in their lives by applying role enrichment strategies.

## Societal Conditions

The modern workplace is increasingly enriched with training programs, educational opportunities for occupational certification, and even opportunities to continue graduate-level education at the company's expense (e.g., Kraiger & Ford, 2007; Rothwell & Kolb, 1999). These training and educational opportunities allow workers to expand their knowledge base in specialty technical topics (e.g., real estate agent becoming certified in home-residential sales) or general organizational topics (e.g., how to negotiate effectively, time management, stress management, effective organizational communication, and budgeting). As such, employees who take advantage of training or educational opportunities learn new skills and accumulate more resources. These work-related skills and resources are easily transferrable to other roles in other life domains resulting in increased life balance.

## Summary and Conclusion

This chapter focused on role enrichment strategies designed to enhance life balance. Role enrichment strategies involve the use of skills, experiences, and resources (proven successful in meeting demand in one role) to meet role demand in another role and thus increase satisfaction in that life domain. Doing so serves to maintain an acceptable level of overall life satisfaction.

There are at least four strategies that characterize role enrichment. These are (1) skills, (2) perspectives, (3) flexibility, and (4) resources – physical, psychological, social, and material. With respect to the skills role enrichment strategy, the use of skills (people skills, coping skills, multitasking skills, etc.) often used in one domain to improve role performance can also be used to improve role performance and increase satisfaction in another domain. The perspectives strategy calls for the adoption of a similar perspective across roles in different life domains – perspectives such as understanding personality differences, valuing cultural diversity, appreciating another person's position on issues, valuing trust, etc. That is, a perspective adopted in a role in a specific life domain that led to successful role performance in that domain could also be adopted to facilitate role performance in another domain. The flexibility strategy is somewhat akin to the perspectives strategy. Applying rules of flexibility (i.e., discretion to determine the timing, pace, and location at which role demand is met) that led to improvement in role performance can also be implemented in another domain. The net result is increased satisfaction in the other domain, which in turn contributes to life satisfaction at large. With respect to the resources strategy, the idea is that applying resources (i.e., psychological, physical, social, and material resources) often used in one domain to improve role performance can also be used to improve role performance in another domain. Doing so serves to increase satisfaction in the other domain.

I then discussed conditions favorable to role enrichment strategies in terms of three sets of factors: situational, personal, and societal. Situational conditions involve increased role demand in a particular life domain. Personal conditions involve individuals high on core self-evaluations. Finally, societal conditions involve increased education and training opportunities.

# PART IV

# Epilogue

This part of the book contains one chapter, namely Chapter 11. The chapter wraps up the book by summing up the key theoretical propositions of life balance and offers the reader a broadened perspective of personal happiness. Specifically, the principles of wellbeing cannot be fully understood and successfully implemented without taking into account the principles of life balance. Life balance is quintessential to wellbeing at large.

# 11 | *Concluding Thoughts*

Life balance is an important concept because understanding this concept can help people enhance their own wellbeing and personal happiness. That is, achieving life balance contributes significantly to happiness. When employees manage to achieve a more balanced life, they become more productive, their job performance improves, they become more committed to their employing organizations, and the morale in those organizations increases, among a host of other positive organizational outcomes. When people experience a more balanced life, they become better citizens, more responsible citizens, and more civically engaged. They become more active in their neighborhoods and communities, which in turn heightens community cohesion and collective problem-solving. They become more politically active and care more about their surroundings, the environment, and the world at large. Achieving a more balanced life is good for people, organizations, communities, society, and humankind in all its wonder and complexity.

People can achieve a more balanced life by manipulating their thoughts and engaging in action that paves the way to life balance and increased wellbeing. This book focused on eight behavioral strategies that balanced individuals commonly use to enhance their subjective wellbeing. I explained how these behavioral strategies life satisfaction through a set of psychological principles. The first three of these strategies are designed to amplify the impact of satisfying life domains on overall life satisfaction, whereas the remaining six strategies are designed to increase domain satisfaction and decrease domain dissatisfaction. As such, I believe that there are two sets of strategic requisites of life balance. One requisite is to prompt greater participation of satisfying life domains to contribute to life satisfaction; the second requisite is to increase domain satisfaction and reduce dissatisfaction. These two strategic requisites result in what we call "life balance."

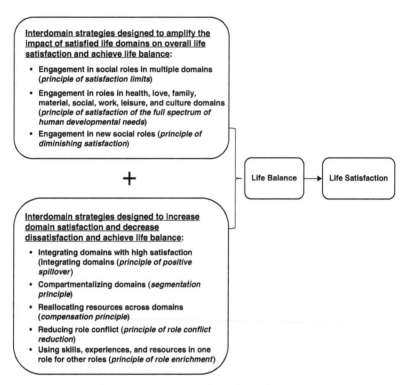

**Figure 11.1** Interdomain strategies to achieve life balance and maintain acceptable levels of life satisfaction

The first three interdomain strategies designed to amplify the impact of satisfied life domains on overall life satisfaction include: (1) engagement in social roles in multiple life domains (explained by the principle of satisfaction limits); (2) engagement in roles in health, safety, economic, social, work, leisure, and cultural domains (explained by the principle of satisfaction of the full spectrum of human development needs); and (3) engagement in new social roles (explained by the principle of diminishing satisfaction). The five interdomain strategies designed to increase domain satisfaction and decrease domain dissatisfaction include: (1) integrating domains with high satisfaction (explained by the principle of positive spillover); (2) compartmentalizing domains with low satisfaction (explained by the segmentation principle); (3) reallocating resources across domains (explained by the compensation principle); (4) stress management (explained by the principle of role conflict); and (5) using skills, experiences, and resources in one role for other roles (explained by the principle of role enrichment). See Figure 11.1.

Though I identified at least eight different strategies – as outlined previously – that were divided into two sets of overarching behavioral principles, I encourage researchers to make a concerted effort to identify more behavioral strategies of life balance within each set. For example, one can argue that people who have a balanced life are adept at organizing their lives. That is, they use organizational skills to help them excel in various social roles across a variety of life domains. This may be a new principle involving the second set of interdomain strategies – strategies designed to increase domain satisfaction and decrease dissatisfaction. Another behavioral strategy that may involve the second set of strategies is efficiency. To be efficient is to try to generate more output than input. Efficiency skills require an individual to be creative when engaging in tasks that manage to produce good results but by employing a different process from the status quo. How about making decisions in one social role in a particular life domain by taking a whole-life perspective – by considering the effect of that decision on satisfaction in other life domains? Could this be a behavioral strategy of the second set (interdomain strategies designed to increase domain satisfaction and decrease dissatisfaction)?

Understanding the dimensions of life balance and the theoretical mechanisms linking life balance with life satisfaction should help practitioners and policymakers formulate programs that can enhance subjective wellbeing. Armed with this greater understanding, therapists, life coaches, human resource managers, and policymakers can develop better programs to help their own constituencies achieve greater balance in their lives.

Back in 2009, I wrote a paper with one of my graduate students (Sirgy & Wu, 2009) that was published in the *Journal of Happiness Studies* that won the best paper award in that journal and was also published elsewhere (Sirgy, 2013). The title of the article was "The Pleasant Life, the Engaged Life, and the Meaningful Life: What about the Balanced Life?" I made the case in that article that the concept of the balanced life is an important concept in the study of personal happiness and wellbeing. Allow me to elaborate.

Martin Seligman, the founder of the positive psychology movement and a guru in the science of happiness and wellbeing, argued that *authentic happiness* has three pillars, namely the pleasant life, the engaged life, and the meaningful life (Seligman, 2002). That is, authentic happiness must involve these three elements. The *pleasant life* is about maximizing feelings of pleasure and minimizing feelings of pain. This is the essence of hedonism captured by momentary experiences of pleasures. The goal in authentic happiness is to ensure a preponderance of positive over negative emotions. Thus, happiness, from the perspective of the pleasant life, is a high level of momentary pleasures – more pleasures than pains. What makes a happy life is, first and foremost, a pleasant life. To maximize happiness, we should pay attention to bodily pleasures and try to increase these pleasures. Seligman advises us to maximize the pleasant life through techniques such as habituation, savoring, and mindfulness. Habituation involves the spreading out of events that produce pleasure far enough in time to generate a craving. For example, go on a fast for half a day instead of constantly snacking. By depriving yourself of food for so long you develop a craving. When you sit down to eat after the fast, the food would taste extra pleasurable. Savoring involves indulging the senses. For example, when you sit down to eat dinner, don't rush through it. Instead, savor the dinner experience – slow down and concentrate on tasting the food and enjoying it. Mindfulness involves becoming acutely aware of the surroundings – focusing on the here and now. By being mindful of the here and now, you can extract more pleasure from the momentary experiences in a given situation. Don't allow your mind to wander by thinking about the past or the future. Concentrate on the present.

*The engaged life* focuses on gratification, not pleasure. It goes beyond hedonism. The engaged life reflects the type of happiness that stems from getting what you want. Fulfillment of a desire contributes to one's happiness regardless of the amount of pleasure (or displeasure) the person may experience. Thus, the criterion for happiness in the engaged life moves from the pleasures of hedonism to the somewhat less subjective state of how well one is engaged or absorbed in life's activities. Seligman provides us with plenty of advice on how to enhance gratification by engaging in activities that generate flow experience – the complete absorption in tasks in ways that elevate subjective wellbeing. Thus, happiness is not only about experiencing pleasure (the pleasant life) but also experiencing desire fulfillment through engagement (the engaged life).

According to Seligman, to experience authentic happiness, the person has to have a *meaningful life* too. That is experiencing a pleasant life is not enough to achieve authentic happiness. Further, it is not enough to experience a pleasant life plus an engaged life. One must experience a meaningful life in conjunction with a pleasant and an engaged life to be "authentically" happy. Happiness comes from achieving worthwhile pursuits such as career accomplishments, meaningful friendships, civic spirit, beauty, education, love, knowledge, and good conscience. Thus, leading a meaningful life is key to happiness. The person who lives a meaningful life is one that serves what is larger and more worthwhile than just the self's pleasures and desires.

In sum, Seligman holds that there are three distinct kinds of happiness: the pleasant life, the engaged life, and the meaningful life. In my 2009 and 2013 publications, I have made the case that Seligman's theory of authentic happiness misses another important criterion of happiness, namely achieving balance in life. That is, to achieve "authentic happiness," people must experience a pleasant life, an engaged life, a meaningful life, *plus* a balanced life. A balanced life is an important requisite for authentic happiness.

# References

Achour, M., Grine, F., & Mohd Nor, M. R. (2014). Work-family conflict and coping strategies: Qualitative study of Muslim female academicians in Malaysia. *Mental Health, Religion, & Culture, 17*, 1002–1014.

Adams, G. A., & Jex, S. M. (1999). Relationships between time management, control, work–family conflict, and strain. *Journal of Occupational Health Psychology, 4*, 72–93.

Ahuvia, A. C., & Friedman, D. C. (1998). Income, consumption, and subjective well-being: Toward a composite macromarketing model. *Journal of Macromarketing, 18*, 153–168.

Ahuvia, A. C., & Wong, N. Y. (2002). Personality and values based materialism: Their relationship and origins. *Journal of Consumer Psychology, 12*, 389–402.

Aldea, M. A., & Rice, K. G. (2006). The role of emotional dysregulation in perfectionism and psychological distress. *Journal of Counseling Psychology, 53*, 498–521.

Alderfer, C. P. (1972). *Existence, relatedness, and growth: Human needs in organizational settings*. New York: The Free Press.

Allen, T. D. (2001). Family-supportive work environments: The role of organizational perceptions. *Journal of Vocational Behavior, 58*, 414–435.

Allen, T. D., & Armstrong, J. (2006). Further examination of the link between work-family conflict and physical health: The role of health-related behaviors. *American Behavioral Scientist, 49*, 1204–1221.

Allen, T. D., Golden, T. D., & Shockley, K. M. (2015). How effective is telecommuting? Assessing the status of our scientific findings. *Psychological Science in the Public Interest, 16*, 40–68.

Allen, T. D., Herst, D. E., Bruck, C. S., & Sutton, M. (2000). Consequences associated with work-to-family conflict: A review and agenda for future research. *Journal of Occupational Health Psychology, 5*, 278–308.

Amabile, T. M. (1993). Motivational synergy: Toward new conceptualizations of intrinsic and extrinsic motivation in the workplace. *Human Resource Management Review, 3*, 185–201.

Andrews, F. M., & Withey, S. B. (1976). *Social indicators of well-being: America's perception of life quality*. New York: Plenum Press.

Ashby, J. S., & Rice, K. G. (2002). Perfectionism, dysfunctional attitudes, and self-esteem: A structural equations analysis. *Journal of Counseling & Development, 80*, 197–203.

Ashforth, B. E., Kreiner, G. E., & Fugate, M. (2000). All in a day's work: Boundaries and micro role transitions. *Academy of Management Review, 25*, 472–491.

Aycan, Z. (2008). Cross-cultural approaches to work-family conflict. In K. Horabik, D. S. Lero, & D. L. Whitehead (Eds.), *Handbook of work-family integration* (pp. 353–370). Cambridge, MA: Academic Press.

Ayman, R., & Antani, A. (2008). Social support and work–family conflict. In K. Korabik, D. S. Lero, & D. L. Whitehead (Eds.), *Handbook of work-family integration: Research, theory and best practices* (pp. 287–304). Amsterdam: Elsevier.

Backman, M. (2020, April 20). Is COVID-19 destroying work-life balance? The ongoing crisis may be changing the way we do our jobs, and not for the better. *The Motley Fool.* www.fool.com/careers/2020/04/25/is-covid-19-destroying-work-life-balance.aspx

Bailey, D. E., & Kurland, N. B. (2002). A review of telework research: Findings, new directions, and lessons for the study of modern work. *Journal of Organizational Behavior, 23*, 383–400.

Baldoma Jones, P. (2020, March 8). 7 reasons why the gig economy is here to stay. *Celerative.* www.celerative.com/blog/7-reasons-why-the-gig-economy-is-here-to-stay

Barsade, S. G. (2002). The ripple effect: Emotional contagion and its influence on group behavior. *Administrative Science Quarterly, 47*, 644–675.

Beauregard, T. A., & Henry, L. C. (2009). Making the link between work-life balance practices and organizational performance. *Human Resource Management Review, 19*, 9–22.

Beehr, T. A., Farmer, S. J., Glazer, S., Gudanowski, D. M., & Nair, V. (2003). The enigma of social support and occupational stress: Source congruence and gender role effects. *Journal of Occupational Health Psychology, 8*, 220–231.

Berger, T., Frey, C. B., Levin, G., & Danda, S. R. (2019). Uber happy? Work and well-being in the 'gig economy'. *Economic Policy, 34*(99), 429–477.

Best, C. J., Cummins, R. A., & Lo, S. K. (2000). The quality of rural and metropolitan life. *Australian Journal of Personality, 52*, 69–74.

Beutell, N. J., & Wittig-Berman, U. (1999). Predictors of work–family conflict and satisfaction with family, job, career, and life. *Psychological Reports, 85*, 893–903.

Bhargava, S. (1995). An integration-theoretical analysis of life satisfaction. *Psychological Studies, 40*, 170–187.

Bosnjak, M., Brown, C. A., Lee, D.-J., Yu, G. B., & Sirgy, M. J. (2016). Self-expressiveness in sport tourism: Determinants and consequences. *Journal of Travel Research, 55*, 125–134.

Boswell, W. R., & Olson-Buchanan, J. B. (2007). The use of communication technologies after hours: The role of work attitudes and work-life conflict. *Journal of Management, 33*, 592–610.

Brief, A. P., Butcher, A. H., George, J. M., & Link, K. E. (1993). Integrating bottom-up and top-down theories of subjective well-being: The case of health. *Journal of Personality and Social Psychology, 64*, 646–667.

Brito, J., & Kassel, G. (2020, February 21). A beginner's guide to open relationships. *Healthline*. www.healthline.com/health/open-relationship

Broadbridge, A. (2000). Stress and the female retail manager. *Women in Management Review, 15*, 145–156.

Broadbridge, A. (2002). Retail managers: Their work stressors and coping strategies. *Journal of Retailing and Consumer Services, 9*, 173–183.

Brush, C. G. (1992). Research on women business owners: Past trends, a new perspective and future directions. *Entrepreneurship Theory and Practice, 16*, 5–30.

Bulger, C. A., & Fisher, G. G. (2012). Ethical imperatives of work/life balance. In N. P. Reilly, M. J. Sirgy, C. A. Gorman (Eds.), *Work and quality of life* (pp. 181–202). Dordrecht, Netherlands: Springer.

Bulger, C. A., Matthews, R. A., & Hoffman, M. E. (2007). Work and personal life boundary management: Boundary strength, work/personal life balance, and the segmentation-integration continuum. *Journal of Occupational Health Psychology, 12*, 365–375.

Butler, A., Gasser, M., & Smart, L. (2004). A social-cognitive perspective on using family-friendly benefits. *Journal of Vocational Behavior, 65*, 57–70.

Byrne, U. (2005). Work-life balance: Why are we talking about it at all? *Business Information Review, 22*, 53–59.

Byron, K. (2005). A meta-analytic review of work-family conflict and its antecedents. *Journal of Vocational Behavior, 67*, 169–198.

Campbell, A., Converse, P. E., & Rodgers, W. L. (1976). *The quality of American life: Perceptions, evaluations, and satisfactions.* New York: Russell Sage Foundation.

Campbell, J. D. (1986). Similarity and uniqueness: The effects of attribution type, relevance, and individual differences in self-esteem and depression. *Journal of Personality and Social Psychology, 50*, 281–294.

Capic, T., Li, N., & Cummins, R. A. (2018). Confirmation of subjective wellbeing set-points: Foundational for subjective social indicators. *Social Indicators Research, 137*, 1–28.

Carlson, D. S., Ferguson, M., & Kacmar, K. M. (2016). Boundary management tactics: An examination of the alignment with preferences in the work and family domains. *Journal of Behavioral and Applied Management*, 16, 1158–1174.

Carlson, D. S., & Frone, M. R. (2003). Relation of behavioral and psychological involvement to a new four-factor conceptualization of work–family interference. *Journal of Business and Psychology*, 17, 515–535.

Carlson, M. C., Parisi, J. M., Xia, J., Xue, Q. L., Rebok, G. W., Bandeen-Roche, K., & Fried, L. P. (2012). Lifestyle activities and memory: Variety may be the spice of life. The women's health and aging study II. *Journal of the International Neuropsychological Society*, 18, 286–294.

Casper, W. J., Eby, L. T., Bordeaux, C., Lockwood, A., & Lambert, D. (2007). A review of research methods in IO/OB work family research. *Journal of Applied Psychology*, 92, 28–43.

Chesley, N. (2005). Blurring boundaries? Linking technology use, spillover, individual distress, and family satisfaction. *Journal of Marriage and Family*, 67, 1237–1248.

Christian, M. S., Garza, A. S., & Slaughter, J. E. (2011). Work engagement: A quantitative review and test of its relations with task and contextual performance. *Personnel Psychology*, 64, 89–136.

Clark, R. A., Nye, F. I., & Gecas, V. (1978). Husbands' work involvement and marital role performance. *Journal of Marriage and the Family*, 40, 9–21.

Clark, S. C. (2000). Work/family border theory: A new theory of work/family balance. *Human Relations*, 53, 747–770.

Clayton, R. W., Thomas, C. H., Singh, B., & Winkel, D. E. (2015). Exercise as a means of reducing perceptions of work-family conflict: A test of the roles of self-efficacy and psychological strain. *Human Resource Management*, 54, 1013–1035.

Cliff, J. E. (1998). Does one size fit all? Exploring the relationship between attitudes towards growth, gender, and business size. *Journal of Business Venturing*, 13, 523–542.

Colbert, A., Yee, N., & George, G. (2016). The digital workforce and the workplace of the future. *Academy of Management Journal*, 59, 731–739.

Colombo, L., Cortese, C. G., & Ghislieri, C. (2013). Professional nurses' work-family conflict: Between organizational demands and resources. *Bollettino Di Psicologia Applicata*, 266, 3–12.

Cook, E. P. (1985). *Psychological androgyny*. New York: Pergamon Press.

Cooper, C. L. (2020). Work-life imbalance: Pandemic disruption places new stresses on women lawyers. American Bar Association, December 18, 2020. www.americanbar.org/groups/diversity/women/publications/perspectives/2021/december/worklife-imbalance-pandemic-disruption-places-new-stresses-women-lawyers/

Cotgrove, S. (1965). The relations between work and nonwork among technicians. *The Sociological Review*, New Series, *13*, 121–129.

Cummins, R. A. (2010). Subjective wellbeing, homeostatically protected mood and depression: A synthesis. *Journal of Happiness Studies*, *11*, 1–17.

Cummins, R. A. (2017). Subjective wellbeing homeostasis. In D. S. Dunn (Ed.), *Oxford bibliographies in psychology* (2nd ed.). New York: Oxford University Press.

Cummins, R. A., Capic, T., Fuller-Tyszkiewicz, M., Hutchinson, D., Olsson, C. A., & Richardson, B. (2018). Why self-report variables inter-correlate: The role of homeostatically protected mood. *Journal of Well-Being Assessment*, *2*, 93–114.

Daley, B. (2021). Work-life balance in a pandemic: A public health issue we cannot ignore. *The Conversation*, February 26, 2021. https://theconversation.com/work-life-balance-in-a-pandemic-a-public-health-issue-we-cannot-ignore-155492

Danna, K., & Griffin, R. W. (1999). Health and well-being in the workplace: A review and synthesis of the literature. *Journal of Management*, *25*, 357–384.

DeGroot, T., & Kiker, D. S. (2003). A meta-analysis of the non-monetary effects of employee health management programs. *Human Resource Management*, *42*, 53–69.

Delle Fave, A. (Ed.). (2013). *The exploration of happiness: Present and future perspectives*. Dordrecht: Springer.

DeMartino, R., & Barbato, R. (2003). Differences between women and men MBA entrepreneurs: Exploring family flexibility and wealth creation as career motivators. *Journal of Business Venturing*, *18*, 815–832.

Demerouti, E., Bakker, A. B., & Schaufeli, W. B. (2005). Spillover and crossover of exhaustion and life satisfaction among dual-earner parents. *Journal of Vocational Behavior*, *67*, 266–289.

Den Dulk, L., & Van Doorne-Huiskes, A. (2007). Social policy in Europe: Its impact on families and work. In R. Crompton et al. (Eds.), *Women, men, work and family in Europe* (pp. 35–57). Basingstoke: Palgrave Macmillan.

Denworth, L. (2020). *Friendship: Evolution, biology, and extraordinary power of life's fundamental bond*. New York: Norton.

Derks, D. (2016). Work-related smartphone use, work-family conflict and family role performance: The role of segmentation preference. *Human Relations*, *69*, 1045–1068.

Derks, D., Bakker, A. B., Peters, P., & van Wingerden, P. (2016). Work-related smartphone use, work-family conflict and family role performance: The role of segmentation preference. *Human Relations*, *69*, 1045–1068.

Diener, E. (1984). Subjective well-being. *Psychological Bulletin*, *75*, 542–575.

Diener, E., & Biswas-Diener, R. (2009). *Happiness: Unlocking the mysteries of psychological wealth*. Malden, MA: Blackwell.

Diener, E., Ng, W., & Tov, W. (2008). Balance in life and declining marginal utility of diverse resources. *Applied Research in Quality of Life*, 3, 277–291.

Diener, E., Suh, E., Lucas, R., & Smith, H. (1999). Subjective well-being: Three decades of research. *Psychological Bulletin*, 125, 276–302.

Dimmock, J., Jackson, B., Podlog, L., & Magaraggia, C. (2013). The effect of variety expectations on interest, enjoyment, and locus of causality in exercise. *Motivation and Emotion*, 37, 146–153.

Drolet, A. (2002). Inherent rule variability in consumer choice: Changing rules for change's sake. *Journal of Consumer Research*, 29, 293–305.

Drummond, S., O'Driscoll, M. P., Brough, P., Kalliath, T., Siu, O. L., Timms, C., Riley, D., Sit, C., & Lo, D. (2017). The relationship of social support with well-being outcomes via work-family conflict: Moderating effects of gender, dependents and nationality. *Human Relations*, 70(5), 544–565.

Dubin, R. (1958). *The world of work: Industrial society and human relations*. Englewood Cliffs, NJ: Prentice-Hall.

Dunne, L. (2017). *Lagom: The Swedish art of balanced living*. London: Running Press Adult.

Dunn, J. C., Whelton, W. J., & Sharpe, D. (2006). Maladaptive perfectionism, hassles, coping, and psychological distress in university professors. *Journal of Counseling Psychology*, 53, 511–523.

Duxbury, L., & Higgins, C. (2003). Work-life conflict in Canada in the New Millennium: A status report. Healthy Communities Division, Health Canada.

Duxbury, L. E., Higgins, C. A., & Mills, S. (1992). After-hours telecommuting and work-family conflict: A comparative analysis. *Information Systems Research*, 3, 173–189.

Duxbury, L. E., Higgins, C. A., & Thomas, D. R. (1996). Work and family environments and the adoption of computer-supported supplemental work-at-home. *Journal of Vocational Behavior*, 49, 1–23.

Eakman, A. M. (2016). A subjectively based definition of life balance using personal meaning in occupation. *Journal of Occupational Science*, 23, 108–127.

Eby, L. T., Casper, W. J., Lockwood, A., Bordeaux, C., & Brinley, A. (2005). Work and family research in IO/OB: Content analysis and review of the literature (1980–2002). *Journal of Vocational Behavior*, 66, 124–197.

Eby, L. T., Maher, C. P., & Butts, M. M. (2010). The intersection of work and family life: The role of affect. *Annual Review of Psychology*, 61, 599–622.

Eddleston, K. A., & Mulki, J. (2017). Toward understanding remote workers' management of work-family boundaries: The complexity of workplace embeddedness. *Group and Organization Management, 42,* 346–387.

Edwards, J. R., & Rothbard, N. P. (2000). Mechanisms linking work and family: Clarifying the relationship between work and family constructs. *Academy of Management Review, 25,* 178–199.

Ellison, C. G. (1990). Family ties, friendships, and subjective well-being among Black Americans. *Journal of Marriage and the Family,* 298–310.

Epstein, C. F., & Kalleberg, A. L. (2004). *Fighting for time: Shifting boundaries of work and social life.* New York: Russell Sage Foundation.

Erickson, B. (2003). Social networks: The value of variety. *Contexts, 2,* 25–31.

Erdwins, C. J., Buffardi, L. C., Casper, W. J., & O'Brien, A. S. (2001). The relationship of women's role strain to social support, role satisfaction, and self-efficacy. *Family Relations, 50,* 230–238.

Etkin, J., & Mogilner, C. (2016). Does variety among activities increase happiness? *Journal of Consumer Research, 43,* 210–229.

Ferguson, M., Carlson, D., & Kacmar, K. M. (2015). Flexing work boundaries: The spillover and crossover of workplace support. *Personnel Psychology, 68,* 581–614.

Fiksenbaum, L. M. (2014). Supportive work-family environments: Implications for work-family conflict and well-being. *The International Journal of Human Resource Management, 25,* 653–672.

Fingerman, K. L., Huo, M., Charles, S. T., & Umberson, D. J. (2020). Variety is the spice of late life: Social integration and daily activity. *The Journals of Gerontology: Series B, 75,* 377–388.

Fogarty, M. P., Rapoport, R., & Rapoport, R. N. (1971). *Sex, career, and family.* Beverly Hills, CA: Sage.

Frederick, D. A., Lever, J., Gillispie, B. J., & Garcia, J. R. (2017). What keeps passion alive? Sexual satisfaction is associated sexual communication, mood setting, sexual variety, oral sex, orgasm, and sex frequency in a national U.S. study. *The Journal of Sex Research, 54,* 186–201.

Freund, A. M., & Baltes, P. B. (2002). Life-management strategies of selection, optimization and compensation: Measurement by self-report and construct validity. *Journal of Personality and Social Psychology, 82,* 642–659.

Friede, A., & Ryan, A. M. (2005). The importance of the individual: How self evaluations influence the work–family interface. In E. E. Kossek & S. J. Lambert (Eds.), *Work and life integration: Organizational, cultural, and individual perspectives* (pp. 193–209). Mahwah, NJ: Lawrence Erlbaum Associates.

Frone, M. R., Russell, M., & Cooper, M. L. (1992). Antecedents and outcomes of work-family conflict: Testing a model of the work-family interface. *Journal of Applied Psychology, 77,* 65–80.

Frone, M. R., Yardley, J. K., & Markel, K. S. (1997). Developing and testing an integrative model of the work–family interface. *Journal of Vocational Behavior, 50,* 145–167.

Frost, R. O., Marten, P., Lahart, C., & Rosenblate, R. (1990). The dimensions of perfectionism. *Cognitive Therapy and Research, 14,* 449–468.

Furnham, A. (1991). Work and leisure satisfaction. In F. Strack, M. Argyle, & N. Schwartz (Eds.), *Subjective well-being* (pp. 235–260). Oxford, UK: Pergamon Press.

Furtado, L., Sobral, F., & Peci, A. (2016). Linking demands to work-family conflict through boundary strength. *Journal of Managerial Psychology, 31,* 1327–1342.

Gable, S. L., Gonzaga, G. C., & Strachman, A. (2006). Will you be there for me when things go right? Supportive responses to positive event disclosures. *Journal of Personality and Social Psychology, 91,* 904–917.

Gajendran, R. S., & Harrison, D. A. (2007). The good, the bad, and the unknown about telecommuting: Meta-analysis of psychological mediators and individual consequences. *Journal of Applied Psychology, 92,* 1524–1541.

Glavin, P., & Schieman, S. (2012). Work-family role blurring and work-family conflict: The moderating influence of job resources and job demands. *Work & Occupations, 39,* 71–98.

Glazebrook, C. K., & Munjas, B. A. (1986). Sex roles and depression. *Journal of Psychosocial Nursing and Mental Health Services, 24,* 8–9.

Golden, A. G., & Geisler, C. (2007). Work-life boundary management and the personal digital assistant. *Human Relations, 60,* 519–551.

Golden, L., & Jorgensen, H. (2002). Time after time: Mandatory overtime in the U.S. economy. *EPI Briefing Paper.* Economic Policy Institute, USA.

Golden, T. D. (2012). Altering the effects of work and family conflict on exhaustion: Telework during traditional and nontraditional work hours. *Journal of Business and Psychology, 27,* 255–269.

Goldstein, B., & Eichhorn, R. L. (1961). The changing protestant ethic: Rural patterns in health, work, and leisure. *American Sociological Review, 26,* 557–565.

Goode, W. (1960). A theory of role strain. *American Sociological Review, 25,* 483–496.

Grace, S. L., Williams, A., Stewart, D. E., & Franche, R. L. (2006). Health-promoting behaviors through pregnancy, maternity leave, and return to work: Effects of role spillover and other correlates. *Women & Health, 43,* 51–72.

Grandey, A. A., & Cropanzano, R. (1999). The conservation of resources model applied to work-family conflict and strain. *Journal of Vocational Behavior, 54*, 350–370.

Greenhaus, J. H., & Allen, T. D. (2011). Work-family balance: A review and extension of the literature. In J. C. Quick & L. E. Tetrick (Eds.), *Handbook of occupational health psychology* (pp. 165–183), 2nd edition. Washington, DC: American Psychological Association.

Greenhaus, J. H., & Beutell, N. J. (1985). Sources of conflict between work and family roles. *Academy of Management Review, 10*, 76–88.

Greenhaus, J. H., & Powell, G. N. (2006). When work and family are allies: A theory of work-family enrichment. *Academy of Management Review, 31*, 72–92.

Grzywacz, J. G., & Carlson, D. S. (2007). Conceptualizing work–family balance: Implications for practice and research. *Advances in Developing Human Resources, 9*, 455–471.

Grzywacz, J. G., & Marks, N. F. (2001). Social inequalities and exercise during adulthood: Toward an ecological perspective. *Journal of Health and Social Behavior, 42*, 202–220.

Haavio-Mannila, E. (1971). Satisfaction with family, work, leisure, and life among men and women. *Human Relations, 24*, 585–601.

Hackman, J. R., & Oldham, G. R. (1974). The job diagnostic survey: An instrument for the diagnosis of jobs and the evaluation of job redesign projects (Technical Report No. AD0779828). Connecticut, New Haven: Yale University New Haven.

Hackman, J. R., & Oldham, G. R. (1976). Motivation through the design of work: Test of a theory. *Organizational Behavior and Human Performance, 16*, 250–279.

Hackman, J. R., Oldham, G. R., Janson, R., & Purdy, K. (1975). A new strategy for job enrichment. *California Management Review, 17*, 57–71.

Halbesleben, J. R. B., Wheeler, A. R., & Rossi, A. M. (2012). The costs and benefits of working with one's spouse: A two sample examination of spousal support. Work-family conflict, and emotional exhaustion in work-linked relationships. *Journal of Organizational Behavior, 33*, 597–615.

Haller, M., & Rosenmayr, L. (1971). The pluri-dimensionality of work commitment. *Human Relations, 24*, 501–518.

Hammer, L. B., Kossek, E. E., Yragui, N. L., Bodner, T. E., Hanson, G. C. (2009). Development and validation of a multidimensional measure of supportive supervisor behaviors (FSSB). *Journal of Management, 35*, 837–856.

Hanson, G. C., & Hammer, L. B. (2006). Development and validation of a multidimensional scale of perceived work-family positive spillover. *Journal of Occupational Health Psychology, 11*, 249–267.

Harackiewicz, J. M., Sansone, C., & Manderlink, G. (1985). Competence, achievement orientation, and intrinsic motivation: A process analysis. *Journal of Personality and Social Psychology, 47*, 287–300.

Hatfield, E., Cacioppo, J. T., & Rapson, R. L. (1994). *Emotional contagion.* Cambridge: Cambridge University Press.

Heilman, M. E., & Chen, J. J. (2003). Entrepreneurship as a solution: The allure of self-employment for women and minorities. *Human Resource Management Review, 13*, 347–364.

Heller, D., & Watson, D. (2005). The dynamic spillover of satisfaction between work and marriage: The role of time, mood and personality. *Journal of Applied Psychology, 90*, 1273–1279.

Helson, H. (1964). Current trends and issues in adaptation-level theory. *American Psychologist, 19*, 26–39.

Herzberg, F. (1966). *Work and the nature of man.* Cleveland: World Pub. Co.

Herzberg, F. (1979). The wise and old turk. *Harvard Business Review, 52*, 70–81.

Hewlett, S., Luce, C., Shiller, P., & Southwell, S. (2005). The hidden brain drain: Off-ramps and on-ramps in women's careers. Harvard Business Review research report.

Higgins, E. T. (1997). Beyond pleasure and pain. *American Psychologist, 52*, 1280–1300.

Hill, E. J., Erickson, J. J., Holmes, E. K., & Ferris, M. (2010). Workplace flexibility, work hours, and work-life conflict: Finding an extra day or two. *Journal of Family Psychology, 24*, 349–358.

Hobfoll, S. E. (1989). Conservation of resources: A new attempt at conceptualizing stress. *American Psychologist, 44*, 513–524.

Hobfoll, S. E. (2001). The influence of culture, community and the nested self in the stress process: Advancing conservation of resources theory. *Applied Psychology: An International Review, 50*, 337–421.

Hobfoll, S. E., & Freedy, J. (1993). Conservation of resources: A general stress theory applied to burnout. In W. B. Schaufeli, C. Maslach, & T. Marek (Eds.), *Professional burnout: Recent developments in theory and research* (pp. 115–133). Philadelphia: Taylor and Francis.

Hofstede, G. (1993). Cultural constraints in management theories. *Academy of Management Perspectives, 7*, 81–94.

Holtgrewe, U. (2014). New new technologies: The future and the present of work in information and communication technology. *New Technology, Work and Employment, 29*, 9–24.

Hsieh, C. M. (2003). Counting importance: The case of life satisfaction and relative domain importance. *Social Indicators Research, 61*, 227–240.

Hudson. (2005). The case for work-life balance: Closing the gap between policy and practice, 20:20 Series. Hudson Global Resources.

Hudson. (2006). The Hudson Report: Employment and HR trends (Jan-March 2006). Part Three. HR Insights-Job-sharing: A Fresh Look at Flexible Working, Australia.

Huws, U., Spencer, N. H., & Joyce, S. (2016). The size and characteristics of the on-demand economy in the UK and Europe. *Economist*, November Issue.

Ilies, R., Wilson, K. S., & Wagner, D. T. (2009). The spillover of daily job satisfaction onto employees' family lives: The facilitating role of work-family integration. *Academy of Management Journal, 52*, 87–102.

Jensen, M. T. (2016). A two-wave cross-lagged study of work-role conflict, work-family conflict and emotional exhaustion. *Scandinavian Journal of Psychology, 57*, 591–600.

Johnson, A. F. (2003). Multiple-role self-efficacy and value attainment: Personal factors that mediate the relationships between levels of work and family involvement and work-family conflict. *Dissertation Abstracts International, 64*, 1494.

Jostell, D., & Hemlin, S. (2018). After hours teleworking and boundary management: Effects on work-family conflict. *Work, 60*, 475–483.

Judge, T. A., Erez, A., Bono, J. E., & Thoresen, C. J. (2003). The core self-evaluation scale: Development of a measure. *Personnel Psychology, 56*, 303–331.

Judge, T. A., Locke, E. A., & Durham, C. C. (1997). The dispositional causes of job satisfaction: A core evaluations approach. *Research in Organizational Behavior, 19*, 151–188.

Judge, T. A., Locke, E. A., Durham, C. C., & Kluger, A. N. (1998). Dispositional effects on job and life satisfaction: The role of core evaluations. *Journal of Applied Psychology, 83*, 17–32.

Judge, T. A., Thoresen, C. J., Bono, J. E., & Patton, G. K. (2001). The job satisfaction–job performance relationship: A qualitative and quantitative review. *Psychological Bulletin, 127*, 376–395.

Judge, T. A., Van Vianen, A. E. M., & De Pater, I. E. (2004). Emotional stability, core self-evaluations, and job outcomes: A review of the evidence and an agenda for future research. *Human Performance, 17*, 325–346.

Kabanoff, B., & O'Brien, G. E. (1982). Relationships between work and leisure attributes across occupational and sex groups in Australia. *Australian Journal of Psychology, 34*, 165–182.

Kahn, B. E. (1995). Consumer variety-seeking among goods and services: An integrative review. *Journal of Retailing and Consumer Services, 2*, 139–148.

Kahn, B. E., & Isen, A. M. (1993). The influence of positive affect on variety seeking among safe, enjoyable products. *Journal of Consumer Research, 22*, 257–270.

Kahn, R. L., Wolfe, D. M., Quinn, R., Snoek, J. D., & Rosenthai, R. A. (1964). *Organizational stress*. New York: Wiley.

Kalliath, T., & Brough, P. (2008). Work-life balance: A review of the meaning of the balance construct. *Journal of Management and Organization*, *14*, 323–327.

Kammeyer-Mueller, J. D., Judge, T. A., & Scott, B. A. (2009). The role of core self-evaluations in the coping process. *Journal of Applied Psychology*, *94*, 177–198.

Kasser, T., & Ryan, R. M. (1993). The dark side of the American Dream: Differential correlates of financial success as a central life aspiration. *Journal of Personality and Social Psychology*, *65*, 410–422.

Kässi, O., & Lehdonvirta, V. (2018). Online labour index: Measuring the online gig economy for policy and research. *Technological Forecasting and Social Change*, *137*, 241–248.

Katz, D., & Kahn, R. L. (1978). *The social psychology of organizations*. New York: Wiley.

Kelliher, C., Richardson, J., & Boiarintseva, G. (2019). All of work? All of life? Reconceptualising work-life balance for the 21st century. *Human Resource Management Journal*, *29*, 97–112.

Kepler, E., & Shane, S. (2007). *Are male and female entrepreneurs really that different?* Washington, DC: Office of Advocacy, US Small Business Administration.

Kiburz, K. M., Allen, T. D., & French, K. A. (2017). Work-family conflict and mindfulness: Investigating the effectiveness of a brief training intervention. *Journal of Organizational Behavior*, *38*, 1016–1037.

Kim, H. S., & Drolet, A. (2003). Choice and self-expression: A cultural analysis of variety-seeking. *Journal of Personality and Social Psychology*, *85*, 373–382.

Kim, J., & Hatfield, E. (2004). Love types and subjective well-being: A cross-cultural study. *Social Behavior and Personality: An International Journal*, *32*, 173–182.

Kim, S., & Hollensbe, E. (2017). Work interrupted: A closer look at work boundary permeability. *Management Research Review*, *40*, 1280–1297.

Kitayama, S., & Markus, H. R. (2000). The pursuit of happiness and the realization of sympathy: Cultural patterns of self, social relations, and well-being. In E. Diener & E. M. Suh (Eds.), *Culture and subjective well-being* (pp. 113–161). Cambridge, MA: The MIT Press.

Knecht, M., Wiese, B. S., & Fruend, A. M. (2016). Going beyond work and family: A longitudinal study on the role of leisure in the work-life interplay. *Journal of Organizational Behavior*, *37*, 1061–1077.

Kossek, E., & Distelberg, B. (2009). Work and family employment policy for a transformed work force: Current trends and themes. In A. Crouter & A. Booth (Eds.), *Work-life policies* (pp. 3–49). Washington, DC: Urban Institute Press.

Kossek, E. E., Lautsch, B. A., & Eaton, S. C. (2006). Telecommuting, control, and boundary management: Correlates of policy use and practice, job control, and work-family effectiveness. *Journal of Vocational Behavior, 68*, 347–367.

Kossek, E., Pichler, S., Bodner, T., & Hammer, L. B. (2011). Workplace social support and work–family conflict: A meta-analysis clarifying the influence of general and work–family specific supervisor and organizational support. *Personnel Psychology, 64*, 289–313.

Kossek, E. E., & Ozeki, C. (1998). Work–family conflict, policies, and the job–life satisfaction relationship: A review and directions for organizational behavior–human resources research. *Journal of Applied Psychology, 83*, 139–155.

Kossek, E. E., Ozeki, C., & Kosier, D. W. (2001). Wellness incentives: Lessons learned about organizational change. *Human Resource Planning, 24*, 24–35.

Kossek, E. E., Ruderman, M. N., Braddy, P. W., & Hannum, K. M. (2012). Work-nonwork boundary management profiles: A person-centered approach. *Journal of Vocational Behavior, 81*, 112–128.

Kraiger, K., & Ford, J. K. (2007). The expanding role of workplace training: Themes and trends influencing training research and practice. *Historical Perspectives in Industrial and Organizational Psychology*, 281–309.

Kreiner, G. E., Hollensbe, E. C., & Sheep, B. L. (2009). Balancing borders and bridges: Negotiating the work-home interface via boundary work tactics. *Academy of Management Journal, 52*, 704–730.

Kurland, N. B., & Bailey, D. E. (1999). The advantages and challenges of working here, there anywhere, and anytime. *Organizational Dynamics, 28*, 53–68.

Kuykendall, L., Lei, X., Zhu, Z., & Hu, X. (2020). Leisure choices and employee well-being: Comparing need fulfilment and well-being during TV and other leisure activities. *Health and Well-Being, 12*, 532–558.

LaBier, D. (2019, January 19). Are open relationships as healthy as monogamous ones? Yes! *Psychology Today*. www.psychologytoday .com/us/blog/the-new-resilience/201901/are-open-relationships-healthy-monogamous-ones-yes

Landerholm, E., & Lowenthal, B. (1993). Adding variety to parent involvement activities. *Early Child Development and Care, 91*, 1–16.

Lapierre, L. M., Van Steenbergen, E. F., Peeters, M. C. W., & Kluwer, E. S. (2016). Juggling work and family responsibilities when involuntarily working more from home: A multiwave study of financial sales professionals. *Journal of Organizational Behavior, 37*, 804–822.

Lay, C. H., & Schouwenburg, H. C. (1993). Trait procrastination, time management. *Journal of Social Behavior and Personality, 8*, 647–662.

Lee, D-J., & Sirgy, M. J. (2017). What do people do to achieve work-life balance? A formative conceptualization to help develop a metric for large-scale quality-of-life surveys. *Social Indicators Research, 138*, 771–791.

Lee, D.-J., Sirgy, M. J., Yu, G. B., & Chalamon, I. (2015). The well-being effects of self-expressiveness and hedonic enjoyment associated with physical exercise. *Applied Research in Quality of Life, 10*, 141–159.

Leiter, M., & Maslach, C. (2005). *Banishing burnout: Six strategies for improving your relationships at work*. San Francisco, CA: Jossey-Bass.

Leslie, L. M., King, E. B., & Clair, J. A. (2019). Work-life ideologies: The contextual basis and consequences of beliefs about work and life. *Academy of Management Review, 44*, 72–98.

Levav, J., & Zhu, R. (2009). Seeking freedom through variety. *Journal of Consumer Research, 36*, 600–610.

Lewicki, P. (1984). Self-schema and social information processing. *Journal of Personality and Social Psychology, 47*, 1177–1190.

Liao, E. Y., Lau, V. P., Hui, R. T., & Kong, K. H. (2019). A resource-based perspective on work-family conflict: Meta-analytical findings. *Career Development International, 24*, 37–73.

Lim, V. K. G., & Chen, D. J. D. (2012). Cyberloafing at the workplace: Gain or drain on work. *Behaviour & Information Technology, 31*, 343–353.

Lim, V. K. G., Teo, S. H., & Loo, G. L. (2002). How do I loaf here? Let me count the ways. *Communication of the ACM, 45*, 66–70.

Liu, J., Kwan, H. K., Lee, C., & Hui, C. (2013). Work-to-family spillover effects of workplace ostracism: The role of work-home segmentation preferences. *Human Resource Management, 52*, 75–94.

Lo, A., & Abbott, M. J. (2013). Review of the theoretical, empirical, and clinical status of adaptive and maladaptive perfectionism. *Behaviour Change, 30*, 96–116.

Lockwood, N. R. (2003). Work-Life Balance: Challenges and Solutions, *SHRM Research Quarterly No 2*. Society for Human Resource Management, USA.

Loscocco, K. A. (1997). Work-family linkages among self-employed women and men. *Journal of Vocational Behavior, 50*, 204–226.

Loscocco, K. A., & Leicht, K. T. (1993). Gender, work-family linkages, and economic success among small business owners. *Journal of Marriage and the Family, 55*, 875–887.

Lucas, R. E., Diener, E., & Suh, E. (1996). Discriminant validity of well-being measures. *Journal of Personality and Social Psychology, 71*, 616–628.

Macan, T. H., Shahani, C., Dipboye, R. L., & Phillips, A. P. (1990). College students' time management: Correlations with academic performance and stress. *Journal of Educational Psychology, 82*, 760–784.

Malone, E. K., & Issa, R. R. (2013). Work-life balance and organizational commitment of women in the US construction industry. *Journal of Professional Issues in Engineering Education and Practice, 139*, 87–98.

Mann, S., & Holdsworth, L. (2003). The psychological impact of teleworking: Stress, emotions and health. *New Technology, Work and Employment, 18*, 196–211.

Maslow, A. H. (1954, 1970). *Motivation and personality.* New York: Harper.

Maslow, A. (1962). *Toward a psychology of being.* New York: Nostrand.

Matuska, K. (2012). Validity evidence of a model and measure of life balance. *Occupation, Participation and Health, 32*, 229–237.

Matthews, R. A., & Barnes-Farrell, J. L. (2010). Development and initial evaluation of an enhanced measure of boundary flexibility for the work and family domains. *Journal of Occupational Health Psychology, 15*, 330–346.

Matthews, R. A., Swody, C. A., & Barnes-Farrell, J. L. (2011). Work hours and work-family conflict: The double-edged sword of involvement in work and family. *Stress and Health, 28*, 234–247,

Matthews, R. A., Winkel, D. E., & Wayne, J. H. (2014). A longitudinal examination of role overload and work-family conflict: The mediating role of interdomain transitions. *Journal of Organizational Behavior, 35*, 72–91.

McAlister, L., & Pessemier, E. (1982). Variety seeking behaviour: An interdisciplinary review. *Journal of Consumer Research, 8*, 311–322.

McDonald, P., & Bradley, L. (2005). The case for work-life balance: Closing the gap between policy and practice. *Hudson Global Resources 20:20 Series.* Hudson: Sydney.

McNall, L. A., Masuda, A. D., Shanock, L. R., & Nicklin, J. M. (2011). Interactive effects of core self-evaluations and perceived organizational support on work-to-family enrichment. *Journal of Psychology: Interdisciplinary & Applied, 145*, 133–149.

McNall, L. A., Nicklin, J. M., & Masuda, A. D. (2010). A meta-analytic review of the consequences associated with work–family enrichment. *Journal of Business and Psychology, 25*, 381–396.

Medrano, L. A., & Trogolo, M. A. (2018). Employee well-being and life satisfaction in Argentina: The contribution of psychological detachment from work. *Journal of Work and Organizational Psychology, 34*, 69–81.

Michel, J. S., & Clark, M. A. (2013). Investigating the relative importance of individual differences on work-family interface and the moderating role of boundary preference for segmentation. *Stress and Health, 29*, 324–336.

Michel, J. S., & Hargis, M. B. (2008). Linking mechanisms of work-family conflict and segmentation. *Journal of Vocational Behavior, 73*, 509–522.

Michel, J. S., Kotrba, L. M., Mitchelson, J. K., Clark, M. A., & Baltes, B. B. (2011). Antecedents of work-family conflict: A meta-analytic review. *Journal of Organizational Behavior, 32,* 689–725.

Michel, J. S., Mitchelson, J. K., Kotrba, L. M., LeBreton, J. M., & Baltes, B. B. (2009). A comparative test of work-family conflict models and critical examination of work-family linkages. *Journal of Vocational Behavior, 74,* 199–218.

Miller, L., & Weiss, R. (1982). The work-leisure relationship: Evidence for the compensatory. *Human Relations, 35,* 763–771.

Myrie, J., & Daly, K. (2009). The use of boundaries by self-employed, home based workers to manage work and family: A qualitative study in Canada. *Journal of Family Economic Issues, 30,* 386–398.

Naithani, P. (2010). Overview of work-life balance discourse and its relevance in current economic scenario. *Asian Social Science, 6,* 148–155.

Naithani, P., & Jha, A. N. (2009). An empirical study of work and family life spheres and emergence of work-life balance initiatives under uncertain economic scenario. *Growth - MTI, 37,* 69–73.

Napholz, L. (2000). Balancing multiple roles among a group of urban middle American Indian working women. *Health Care for Women International, 21,* 255–266.

Neck, C. P., & Cooper, K. H. (2000). The fit executive: Exercise and diet guidelines for enhancing performance. *Academy of Management Executive, 14,* 72–83.

Netemeyer, R. G., Boles, J. S., & McMurrian, R. (1996). Development and validation of work-family conflict and family-work conflict scales. *Journal of Applied Psychology, 81,* 400–410.

Neumann, R., & Strack, F. (2000). "Mood contagion": The automatic transfer of mood between persons. *Journal of Personality and Social Psychology, 79,* 211–224.

Nippert-Eng, C. E. (1996). *Home and work.* Chicago, IL: The University of Chicago Press.

OECD. (2001). Balancing work and family life: Helping parents into paid employment. In *OECD employment outlook 2001* (pp. 29–166). Paris: OECD.

OECD. (2007). *Babies and bosses, reconciling work and family Life: A synthesis of findings for OECD countries.* Paris: OECD.

Olson-Buchanan, J., & Boswell, W. R. (2006). Blurring boundaries: Correlates of integration and segmentation between work and non-work. *Journal of Vocational Behavior, 68,* 432–445.

Oppewal, H., Timmermans, H. J., & Louviere, J. J. (1997). Modelling the effects of shopping centre size and store variety on consumer choice behaviour. *Environment and Planning, 29,* 1073–1090.

Ozbilir, T., Day, A., & Catano, V. M. (2015). Perfectionism at work: An investigation of adaptive and maladaptive perfectionism in the workplace among Canadian and Turkish employees. *Applied Psychology, 64,* 252–280.

Ozer, E. M. (1995). The impact of childcare responsibility and self-efficacy on the psychological health of professional working mothers. *Psychology of Women Quarterly, 19,* 315–335.

Parasuraman, S., Purohit, Y. S., Godshalk, V. M., & Beutell, N. J. (1996). Work and family variables, entrepreneurial career success, and psychological well-being. *Journal of Vocational Behavior, 48,* 275–300.

Parasuraman, S., & Simmers, C. A. (2001). Type of employment, work–family conflict and well-being: A comparative study. *Journal of Organizational Behavior, 22,* 551–568.

Park, H. J., Heppner, P. P., & Lee, D. G. (2010). Maladaptive coping and self-esteem as mediators between perfectionism and psychological distress. *Personality and Individual Differences, 48,* 469–474.

Park, Y., Fritz, C., & Jex, S. M. (2011). Relationships between work-home segmentation and psychological detachment from work: The role of communication technology use at home. *Journal of Occupational Health Psychology, 16,* 457–469.

Parks, K. M., & Steelman, L. A. (2008). Organizational wellness programs: A meta-analysis. *Journal of Occupational Health Psychology, 13,* 58–68.

Percheski, C. (2008). Opting out? Cohort differences in professional women's employment rates from 1960 to 2005. *American Sociological Review, 73,* 497–517.

Perrone, K. M., & Civiletto, C. L. (2004). The impact of life role salience on life satisfaction. *Journal of Employment Counseling, 41,* 105–117.

Pierce, J. L., & Dunham, R. B. (1976). Task design: A literature review. *Academy of Management Review, 1,* 83–97.

Piszczek, M. M. (2017). Boundary control and controlled boundaries: Organizational expectations for technology use at the work-family interface. *Journal of Organizational Behavior, 38,* 592–611.

Piszczek, M. M., DeArmond, S., & Feinauer, D. (2018). Employee work-to-family role boundary management in the family business. *Community, Work, & Family, 21,* 111–132.

Pollock, A. S., Durward, B. R., Rowe, P. J., & Paul, J. P. (2000). What is balance? *Clinical Rehabilitation, 14,* 402–406.

Powell, G. N., & Eddleston, K. A. (2013). Linking family-to-business enrichment and support to entrepreneurial success: Do female and male entrepreneurs experience different outcomes? *Journal of Business Venturing, 28,* 261–280.

Preusser, K. J., Rice, K. G., & Ashby, J. S. (1994). The role of self-esteem in mediating the perfectionism-depression connection. *Journal of College Student Development, 15,* 205–230.

Rain, J. S., Lane, I. M., & Steiner, D. D. (1991). A current look at the job satisfaction/life satisfaction relationship: Review and future considerations. *Human Relations, 44*, 287–307.

Rapoport, R., Rapoport, R., & Thiessen, V. (1974). Couple symmetry and enjoyment. *Journal of Marriage and the Family, 36*, 588–591.

Ratner, R. K., Kahn, B. E., & Kahneman, D. (1999). Choosing less preferred experiences for the sake of variety. *Journal of Consumer Research, 26*, 1–15.

Rice, R. W., McFarlin, D. B., Hunt, R. G., & Near, J. P. (1985). Organizational work and the perceived quality of life: Toward a conceptual model. *Academy of Management Review, 10*, 296–310.

Richins, M. L., & Dawson, S. (1992). A consumer values orientation for materialism and its measurement: Scale development and validation. *Journal of Consumer Research, 19*, 303–316.

Richins, M. L., & Rudmin, F. W. (1994). Materialism and economic psychology. *Journal of Economic Psychology, 15*, 217–231.

Roberts, J. A., & Clement, A. (2007). Materialism and satisfaction with overall quality of life and eight life domains. *Social Indicators Research, 82*, 79–92.

Rojas, M. (2006). Life satisfaction and satisfaction in domains of life: Is it a simple or a simplified relationship? *Journal of Happiness Studies, 7*, 467–497.

Roos, E., Sarlio-Lähteenkorva, S., Lallukka, T., & Lahelma, E. (2007). Associations of work-family conflicts with food habits and physical activity. *Public Health Nutrition, 10*, 222–229.

Rosenberg, M. (1979). *Conceiving the self*. New York: Basic Books.

Rothwell, W. J., & Kolb, J. A. (1999). Major workforce and workplace trends influencing the training and development field in the USA. *International Journal of Training and Development, 3*, 44–53.

Sanjeev, M. A., & Surya, A. V. (2016). Two factor theory of motivation and satisfaction: An empirical verification. *Annals of Data Science, 3*, 155–173.

Sargent, A. G. (1981). *The androgynous manager*. New York: AMACOM.

Sayer, L. C. (2005). Gender, time and inequality: Trends in women's and men's paid work, unpaid work and free time. *Social Forces, 84*, 285–303.

Schaufeli, W. B., Salanova, M., Gonzalez-Roma, V., & Bakker, A. B. (2002). The measurement of engagement and burnout: A two sample confirmatory factor analytic approach. *Journal of Happiness Studies, 3*, 71–92.

Schaufeli, W. B., & Bakker, A. B. (2004). Job demands, job resources and their relationship with burnout and engagement: A multi-sample study. *Journal of Organizational Behavior, 25*, 293–315.

Schieman, S., & Glavin, P. (2008). Trouble at the border? Gender, flexible work conditions, and the work-home interface. *Social Problems, 55*, 590–611.

Schieman, S., & Young, M. C. (2013). Are communications about work outside regular working hours associated with work-to-family conflict, psychological distress and sleep problems? *Work & Stress, 27,* 244–261.

Scollon, C. N., & Diener, E. (2006). Love, work, and changes in extraversion and neuroticism over time. *Journal of Personality and Social Psychology, 91,* 1152–1165.

Scott, W. A., & Stumpf, J. (1984). Personal satisfaction and role-performance: Subjective and social aspects of adaptation. *Journal of Personality and Social Psychology, 47,* 812–827.

Seligman, M. E. P. (2002). *Authentic happiness: Using the new positive psychology to realize your potential for lasting fulfilment.* New York: The Free Press.

Shane, J., & Heckhausen, J. (2016). Optimized engagement across life domains in adult development: Balancing diversity and interdomain consequences. *Research in Human Development, 13,* 280–296.

Shanine, K. K., Eddleston, K. A., & Combs, J. G. (2019). Same boundary management preference, different outcome: Toward a gendered perspective of boundary theory among entrepreneurs. *Journal of Small Business Management, 57,* 185–205.

Shea, J. R., Spitz, R. S., & Zeller, F. A. (1970). Dual careers: A longitudinal study of labor market experience of women (Vol. 1). Manpower Research Monograph No. 21. Washington, DC: U.S. Government Printing Office.

Sheldon, K. M., Cummins, R., & Kamble, S. (2010). Life balance and well-being: Testing a novel conceptual and measurement approach. *Journal of Personality, 78,* 1093–1134.

Sheldon, K. M., & Niemiec, C. P. (2006). It's not just the amount that counts: Balanced need satisfaction also affects well-being. *Journal of Personality and Social Psychology, 91,* 331–341.

Shepard, J. M. (1974). A status recognition model of work-leisure relationships. *Journal of Leisure Research, 6,* 58–63.

Simonson, I. (1989). Choice based on reasons: The case of attraction and compromise effects. *Journal of Consumer Research, 16,* 158–174.

Simon, M., Kimmerling, A., & Hasselhorn, H. (2004). Work-home conflict in the European nursing profession. *International Journal of Occupational and Environmental Health, 10,* 384–391.

Simonson, I. (1990). The effect of purchase quantity and timing on variety seeking behavior. *Journal of Marketing Research, 27,* 150–162.

Sirgy, M. J. (1998). Materialism and quality of life. *Social Indicators Research, 43,* 227–260.

Sirgy, M. J. (2002). *The psychology of quality of life.* Dordrecht: Kluwer.

Sirgy, M. J. (2012). *The psychology of quality of life: Hedonic well-being, life satisfaction, and eudaimonia.* Dordrecht: Springer.

Sirgy, M. J. (2013). The pleasant life, the engaged life, and the meaningful life: What about the balanced life? In A. D. Fave (Eds.), *The exploration of happiness* (pp. 175–192). Dordrecht: Springer.

Sirgy, M. J. (2019). Positive balance: A hierarchical perspective of positive mental health. *Quality of Life Research, 28,* 1921–1930.

Sirgy, M. J. (2020). *Positive balance: A theory of well-being and positive mental health.* Cham, Switzerland: Springer Nature Switzerland AG.

Sirgy, M. J., Cole, D., Kosenko, R., Meadow, H. L., Rahtz, D., Cicic, M., Jin, G. X., Yarsuvat, D., Blenkhorn, D. L., & Nagpal, N. (1995). Developing a life satisfaction measure based on need hierarchy theory. In M. J. Sirgy & A. C. Samli (Eds.), *New dimensions of marketing and quality of life* (pp. 3–26). Westport, CT: Greenwood Press.

Sirgy, M. J., & Lee, D.-J. (2016). Work-life balance: A quality-of-life model. *Applied Research in Quality of Life, 11,* 1059–1082.

Sirgy, M. J., & Lee, D.-J. (2018). Work-life balance: An integrative review. *Applied Research in Quality of Life, 13,* 229–254.

Sirgy, M. J., Reilly, N., Wu, J., & Efraty, D. (2008). A work-life identity model of well-being: Towards a research agenda linking quality-of-work-life (QWL) programs with quality of life (QOL). *Applied Research in Quality of Life, 3,* 181–202.

Sirgy, M. J., & Wu, J. (2009). The pleasant life, the engaged life, and the meaningful life: What about the balanced life? *Journal of Happiness Studies, 10,* 183–196.

Slan-Jerusalim, R., & Chen, C. P. (2009). Work-family conflict and career development theories: A search for helping strategies. *Journal of Counseling & Development, 87,* 492–500.

Slaney, R. B., Rice, K. G., Mobley, M., Trippi, J., & Ashby, J. S. (2001). The revised almost perfect scale. *Measurement and Evaluation in Counselling and Development, 34,* 130–145.

Sonnentag, S. (2012). Psychological detachment from work during leisure time the benefits of mentally disengaging from work. *Current Directions in Psychological Science, 21,* 114–118.

Sonnentag, S., Mojza, E. J., Binnewies, C., & Scholl, A. (2008). Being engaged at work and detached at home: A week-level study on work engagement, psychological detachment, and affect. *Work & Stress, 22,* 257–276.

Spector, P., Allen, T. D., Poelmans, S. A. Y., Cooper, C. L., Bernin, P., Hart, P. M., ... Yu, S. (2005). An international comparative study of work-family stress and occupational strain. In S. A. Y. Poelmans (Ed.), *Work and family: An international research perspective* (pp. 71–87). London: Lawrence Erlbaum.

Staines, G. L. (1980). Spillover versus compensation. A review of the literature on the relationship between work and nonwork. *Human Relations, 33,* 111–129.

Swan, A. A. (2016). Masculine, feminine, or androgynous: The influence of gender identity on job satisfaction among female police officers. *Women & Criminal Justice, 26,* 1–19.

Sylvester, B. D., Standage, M., McEwan, D., Wolf, S. A., Lubans, D. R., Eather, N., ... Beauchamp, M. R. (2016). Variety support and exercise adherence behavior: Experimental and mediating effects. *Journal of Behavioral Medicine, 39,* 214–224.

Tait, M., Padgett, M. Y., & Baldwin, T. T. (1989). Job and life satisfaction: A reevaluation of the strength of the relationship and gender effects as a function of the date of the study. *Journal of Applied Psychology, 74,* 502–519.

Telfer, E. (1989). The unity of the moral virtues in Aristotle's "Nicomachean Ethics." *Proceedings of the Aristotelian Society, 90,* 35–48.

Thompson, C. A., Beauvais, L. L., & Lyness, K. S. (1999). When work–family benefits are not enough: The influence of work–family culture on benefit utilization, organizational attachment, and work–family conflict. *Journal of Vocational Behavior, 54,* 392–415.

Tian, K. T., Bearden, W. O., & Hunter, G. L. (2001). Consumers' need for uniqueness: Scale development and validation. *Journal of Consumer Research, 28,* 50–66.

Urs, L., & Schmidt, A. M. (2018). Work-family conflict among IT specialty workers in the US. *Community, Work, & Family, 21,* 247–271.

Van Emmerik, H., Bakker, A. B., Westman, M., & Peeters, M. C. W. (2015). Spillover and crossover processes: Consequences for work-life balance. In S. G. Baugh & S. E. Sullivan (Eds.), *Striving for balance* (pp. 97–111). Charlotte, NC: Information Age Publishing, Inc.

van Steenbergen, E. F., Ellemers, N., & Mooijaart, A. (2007). How work and family can facilitate each other: Distinct types of work–family facilitation and outcomes for women and men. *Journal of Occupational Health Psychology, 12,* 279–300.

van Eerde, W., & Klingsieck, K. B. (2018). Overcoming procrastination? A meta-analysis of intervention studies. *Educational Research Review, 25,* 73–85.

Voydanoff, P. (2004). Implications of work and community demands and resources for work-to-family conflict and facilitation. *Journal of Occupational Health Psychology, 9,* 275–285.

Voydanoff, P. (2005a). Consequences of boundary-spanning demands and resources for work-to-family conflict and perceived stress. *Journal of Occupational Health Psychology, 10,* 491–503.

Voydanoff, P. (2005b). The differential salience of family and community demands and resources for family-to-work conflict and facilitation. *Journal of Family Economic Issues, 26,* 395–417.

Voydanoff, P. (2006). *Work, family and community: Exploring interconnections*. Mahwah, NJ: Lawrence Erlbaum Associates.

Walker, K., & Woods, M. (1976). *Time use: A measure of household production of family goods and services*. Washington, DC: American Home Economics Association.

Wang, X., Gao, L., & Lin, Z. (2019). Help or harm? The effects of ICTs usage on work-life balance. *Journal of Managerial Psychology, 34*, 533–545.

Watson, D. (2000). Basic problems in positive mood regulation. *Psychological Inquiry, 11*, 205–209.

Watson, D., Clark, L. A., & Tellegen, A. (1988). Development and validation of brief measures of positive and negative affect: The PANAS scales. *Journal of Personality and Social Psychology, 54*, 1063–1079.

Watson, N. (2002). Happy companies make happy investments. *Fortune Magazine*, May 27.

Wayne, S. J., Lemmon, G., Hoobler, J. M., Cheung, G. W., & Wilson, M. S. (2017). The ripple effect: A spillover model of the detrimental impact of work-family conflict on job success. *Journal of Organizational Behavior, 38*, 876–894.

Wegge, J., Schmidt, K., Parkes, C., & Van Dick, R. (2007). 'Taking a sickie': Job satisfaction and job involvement as interactive predictors of absenteeism in a public organization. *Journal of Occupational & Organizational Psychology, 80*, 77–89.

Weisman, C. (2020). Are open relationships and non-monogamous relationships really that common? *Fatherly*, June 23, 2020. www.fatherly .com/love-money/how-common-open-relationship-non-monogamous-relationships/

Westman, M., Brough, P., & Kalliath, T. (2009). Expert commentary on work-life balance and crossover of emotions and experiences: Theoretical and practice advancements. *Journal of Organizational Behavior, 30*, 587–595.

Westring, A. F., & Ryan, A. M. (2010). Personality and inter-role conflict and enrichment: Investigating the mediating role of support. *Human Relations, 63*, 1815–1834.

Wiese, B. S., Seiger, C. P., Schmid, C. M., & Freund, A. M. (2010). Beyond conflict: Functional facets of the work–family interplay. *Journal of Vocational Behaviour, 77*, 104–117.

Wierda-Boer, H. H., Gerris, J. R., & Vermulst, A. A. (2008). Adaptive strategies, gender ideology, and work-family balance among Dutch dual earners. *Journal of Marriage and Family, 70*, 1004–1014.

Wight, V. R., & Raley, S. B. (2009). When home becomes work: Work and family time among workers at home. *Social Indicators Research, 93*, 197–202.

Williams, J. C., Berdahl, J. L., & Vandello, J. A. (2016). Beyond work-life "integration." *Annual Review of Psychology, 67,* 515–539.

Wilensky, H. (1960). Work, careers, and social integration. *International Social Science Journal, 12,* 543–560.

Wright, N. D., & Larsen, V. (1993). Materialism and life satisfaction: A meta-analysis. *Journal of Consumer Satisfaction, Dissatisfaction, and Complaining Behavior, 6,* 5–27.

Wu, C.-H. (2009). Enhancing quality of life by shifting importance perception among life domains. *Journal of Happiness Studies, 10,* 37–47.

Xin, J., Chen, S., Kwan, H. K., Chiu, R. K., & Yim, F. H. (2018). Work-family spillover and crossover effects of sexual harassment: The moderating role of work-home segmentation preference. *Journal of Business Ethics, 147,* 619–629.

Yang, H., & Chen, J. (2016). Learning perfectionism and learning burnout in a primary school student sample: A test of a learning-stress mediation model. *Journal of Child and Family Studies, 25,* 345–353.

Yang, N. (2005). Individualism-collectivism and work-family interfaces: A Sino-U.S. comparison. In S. A. Y. Poelman (Ed.), *Work and family: An international research perspective* (pp. 229–253). Milton Park, Oxfordshire: Taylor & Francis Group.

Yang, N., Chen, C., Choi, J., & Zou, Y. (2000). Sources of work-family conflict: A Sino-US comparison of the effects of work and family demands. *Academy of Management Journal, 43,* 113–123

Yasbek, P. (2004). The business case for firm-level work-life-balance policies: A review of the literature. Labor Market Policy Group. Wellington: Department of Labour. http://www.dol.govt.nz/PDFs/FirmLevelWLB.pdf

Yeandle, S., Bennett, C., Buckner, L., Shipton, L., & Suokas, A. (2006). Who cares wins: The social and business benefits of supporting working carers. Carers U.K.

Zedeck, S. (1992). *Work, families, and organizations.* San Francisco: Jossey-Bass.

Zedeck, S., & Mosier, K. (1990). Work in the family and employing organization. *American Psychologist, 45,* 240–251.

Zhao, K., Zhang, M., Kaimer, M. L., & Yang, B. (2017). Source attribution matters: Mediation and moderation effects in the relationship between work-to-family conflict and job satisfaction. *Journal of Organizational Behavior, 40,* 492–505.

# Index

Lightning Source UK Ltd.
Milton Keynes UK
UKHW022025030522
402459UK00012B/243